SURVIVING MERGER AND ACQUISITION

SURVIVING
MERGER
AND
ACQUISITION

MICHAEL L. MCMANUS
MICHAEL L. HERGERT

Scott, Foresman and Company

Glenview, Illinois   London

ISBN 0-673-18854-X

Copyright © 1988 Scott, Foresman and Company.

Library of Congress Cataloging-in-Publication Data

McManus, Michael L.
  Surviving merger and acquisition.

  Bibliography: p.
  Includes index.
  1. Organizational change—Management.
2. Consolidation and merger of corporations—Management.
3. Corporate reorganizations—Management.   I. Hergert, Michael
Lee.   II. Title.
HD58.8.M36   1988   658.1′6   87-35643

1 2 3 4 5 6   RRC   93 92 91 90 89 88

Scott, Foresman Professional Publishing Group books are available
for bulk sales at quantity discounts. For information, please contact
the Marketing Manager, Professional Books, Professional Publishing Group, Scott, Foresman and Company, 1900 East Lake Avenue,
Glenview, IL 60025.

PREFACE

Mergers, acquisitions, leveraged buyouts, and bankruptcies have transformed the corporate landscape. Not since the Great Depression have the lives of so many been changed by the dealings of so few. Millions of employees and managers worldwide have been forced to change jobs, occupations, locations, and careers. Millions more will be affected in the last of the eighties and nineties.

The human toll from corporate change can be dramatic—firings, loss of earnings, pensions, and the camaraderie of a workplace. And corporations undergo a battering process as well. After merger and acquisition, they change size, location, style, and sometimes whole areas of business. At the personal level, the pain and dislocation can be very real and immediate. Homes are sold, families are moved, and a sense of identity based on years of affiliation may be lost forever. The obvious changes are the ones seen and talked about. And these are bad enough. But this is where the "good news" begins.

For millions, the upheaval of the merger age has produced a far subtler challenge. For those who properly manage the process of corporate transformation, there is

v

the opportunity for personal growth and advancement. It is more than a silver lining. Simply, we must survive, and go on and learn. However, not everyone will emerge a winner. A passive approach to participation in the merger age can have devastating results.

It is the age of corporate chaos. Too long have our classrooms assumed rational models and rules of the business game. We have written this book because we believe it is important to start a discussion in many classrooms, boardrooms, and living rooms about the causes and effects of corporate restructuring. We intend to give our readers tools and, more than anything else, hope and understanding about what is going on. The events described in the following pages are terribly real and frightening to millions, yet have the potential for stimulating growth. People can, with sufficient vision, rebuild companies and the social and moral character within.

A new priority has emerged for many corporate leaders—a deeper *understanding* of corporate character as a national management issue and as an emerging national political agenda. How can we talk about re-building corporate character if we never knew what it was in the first place? How can we seek corporate integrity if none exists in our daily corporate dealings? This book is not meant to moralize, but it will ask the reader to assess these matters in order to understand the personal meaning of all the changes.

Corporate restructuring will continue; this is a force outside our sphere of influence, for most of us. Yet we can make a difference: it is crucial to respond to the challenge of reshaping corporate character in the days and months after the shock. Middle-managers must develop a new sense of crisis management skills, a sense of human priorities, a sense of personal integrity and political survival skills. They must keep the ship afloat in the stormy seas following corporate restructuring.

There is a great need to analyze corporate culture in a different light—many MBAs, corporate yuppies, and critics have overdosed on the "excellence" craze. Seventy thousand new MBAs will graduate from the classroom in 1987 alone. There is a need to analyze corporate restructuring and transformation beyond what we now have in the textbooks and many of the cases. Many of the best students are confused about how to approach corporate life, and they do not know whether to value or avoid the notion of continuity and stability. And, sadly, many do not know how to help others in crisis, though they see the need. Cornell University Professor Lawrence K. Williams has urged a curriculum of organizational triage* as part of the new-age awareness for training managers. Though not written as a handbook in that vein, this book is a step in that direction. It examines some of the broad impacts of the merger and acquisition trend. It is about personal survival and rebuilding. And it suggests a philosophy and set of skills for helping others as well as self.

---

*In hospital emergency rooms, triage is the system for assigning a priority sequence for treatment of sick and injured when insufficient resources are present.

The ideas and vignettes come mostly from our day-to-day consulting experiences and our study of prior research in the area of mergers and acquisitions. Some of our hardest learning experiences in the consulting "trenches" are our best and most vivid human cases for illustration. We have given the book a traditional mix of references from academic sources as well as current issues from the popular press and media.

We have benefited greatly from editorial suggestions and inputs from our colleagues, including Edgar Schein, Lawrence K. Williams, and Philip R. Harris. In recent years, Harris in particular has concentrated on the notion of corporate synergy and the hope and potential for constructive change. His work and optimism are inspiring. The entire manuscript was polished and greatly improved by Robin Hergert. Her editorial and communication skills were crucial to getting our thoughts onto paper. Robin was a master in helping us to better tell a story that must be told.

We are grateful for the help and faith of our editor, Amy Davis, throughout the process of taking this book from original concept through several merger–acquisition hurdles to final product. She had a sustaining belief that this book has an important enough message for American business students, managers, and leaders to warrant all of her care. It is itself a quintessential testament to the notion that good people can get things through thorny wickets—in the best, or even in the most chaotic of times!

San Diego

CONTENTS

CHAPTER 1
Welcome to the Age of Corporate Chaos | 1

CHAPTER 2
The Turf: Basic Concepts
in Organizational Dynamics | 9

CHAPTER 3
Eagles, Planners, Culture Club:
Schools of Thought on Corporate Chaos | 35

CHAPTER 4
The Players and the Arenas | 59

CHAPTER 5
The How and Why of Empire Building | 83

CHAPTER 6
The Other Side of Merger Mania:
Breaking Up Is Hard to Do | 111

CHAPTER 7
Impact: The Company and Its Parts | 129

CHAPTER 8
Impact: The Human Dimension | 161

CHAPTER 9
Is There Life after Merger Mania? | 185

CHAPTER 10
Where Do We Go from Here? | 207

APPENDICES | 213

GLOSSARY | 225

REFERENCES | 233

INDEX | 241

1

WELCOME TO THE AGE OF CORPORATE CHAOS

The rules of the game have changed. The American corporate scene is being dramatically restructured by a series of mergers, acquisitions, bankruptcies, divestitures, and reorganizations. Sometimes brutal, always subtle, these winds of corporate and organizational change sway fortunes, propel careers, and burst dreams. These forces are inevitable in an advanced economic system, yet few understand their own role in the drama that plays out.

"DON'T GO DOWN THE CELLAR"

Those sad words were the warning that Chris Donahue left for his family in his suicide note. Donahue hanged himself in the cellar just four days after losing his $63,000 per year job at Heublein, Inc. Heublein had recently been acquired by R. J. Reynolds, and Donahue had expected a promotion to Reynolds' headquarters. Instead of a promotion, Donahue got a pink slip and 11 weeks severance pay. Donahue's note went on to say, "Tell someone at RJR that I loved their generosity and compassion . . . They owed me more—the first-class f——ers. I know you will think I failed, and maybe I did. . . . I didn't have the strength to endure the pain that was coming."[1]

Behind the headlines of acquisitions and divestitures lies a wake of human tragedy. Perhaps not many suffer the fate of Chris Donahue, but literally millions of workers have felt the shockwaves of mergers and acquisitions. *Fortune* magazine estimates that in 1983, the ten largest of the 1,500 mergers during that year changed the lives of up to 220,000 employees.

The forces of corporate change are sometimes predictable, but only if we know what to look for. Some corporate planners and investors strive to anticipate changes and will risk great resources on what will result. The enormity of the stakes creates nearly unlimited opportunity—and risk—for those who play.

However, upheavals do not affect just top management and wealthy arbitrageurs. A typical employee spends over one-third of his or her waking hours at work. For many of us, this time is spent at a large corporation. The modern corporation has become a critical social, as well as economic, institution in the lives of many Americans. Yet despite its enormous impact on the quality of life, the corporation is poorly understood by most of its employees. Whenever a company experiences a drastic change, the effects will ripple throughout the organization and can change the lives of every single employee.

In this book, we shall discuss what happens when corporations are hit by a major shock. This includes the growth, decline, and adaptive processes of corporations that dictate:

> . . . if the company will survive long enough to provide a viable job or employment,
>
> . . . if the firm will acquire other companies and improve its performance,
>
> . . . if the corporate entity will merge with another, resulting in some new or "forced" corporate culture,
>
> . . . if the company will be raided and "stripped" of its value (or valuable people),
>
> . . . if the company has a chance of going public, enabling some to realize great gains, or
>
> . . . if the company will become a pawn in a larger international game.

Such processes are the natural cycles that all organizations follow, the universal cycles of growth, decline, adaptation. This is the essence of *corporate destiny*. In this book, we shall attempt to translate what these changes mean for the people who must live through them, and how one can best survive in an era of turmoil.

THE COMMON DENOMINATOR

All of the phenomena described above share a common thread. Takeovers, bankruptcies, leveraged buyouts, and public offerings are all sources of trauma to a firm. The psychological condition pervading organizations that participate in these activities is best described as *corporate chaos*. The atmosphere of the organization is likely to exhibit significant confusion, high anxiety, poor morale, high employee turnover, and many other unintended side effects of organizational change.

The elite corps of raiders and deal-makers who are the driving force behind corporate restructurings have become as visible as movie stars or top athletes. These leaders can exert power to create the scenarios of fundamental change. If a company is heading for a winning-destiny scenario, this will trickle down into personal success and job satisfaction for those whose lives are affected. Unfortunately, as in the case of Chris Donahue, the opposite is also true. How can we learn to discriminate between a likely success scenario and a disaster scenario? What happens and what does it look like? What signs should one look for?

These are the central survival issues that confront us as we delve into the subject of this book . . . corporate chaos . . . how to understand it, how to manage through it, and how to avoid losing propositions and outcomes. Through a conceptual framework and carefully selected cases and vignettes, the authors will guide the reader through the key cycles we are talking about:

¶ Acquisition, merger, buying out, joint ventures (in other words, the processes of blending and melding corporate cultures)

¶ Going public, or the "big bang" approach to corporate and personal success

¶ Restructuring and overhauling corporate entities

¶ Bankruptcy and "going under" strategies

In each of the above situations, there are identifiable patterns of corporate culture dynamics. These will be examined along with the likely winners and the losers for each scenario.

Despite the tremendous power with which these forces operate, not everyone is a passive observer of corporate chaos. For example, executives need specific guidelines and approaches to assist them in *managing* (not just reacting to) organizational change. For this reason, we have studied the strategies of leading managers to see how they deal with corporate chaos and to extract some lessons for others who find themselves in similar situations. Not all of the vignettes are success stories. Dealing with chaos is partly science, but mostly art. However, the financial and human stakes are simply too great to leave outcomes up to chance. Although it is difficult to anticipate exactly how a firm's destiny will unfold, the risks are too high to simply ignore the future and hope for the best.

Many management experts have agreed that it is easier to diagnose the failures and the big mistakes than to explain the successes. Many variables combine, after all, to produce the successful outcomes. One of our missions should be, however, abundantly clear. We shall attempt to educate and sensitize the reader to the role of chaos and to its nearness and ubiquity in the evolution and destiny of corporations.

Doing "business as usual" is a good description of the corporate mentality for the better part of this century. But today, much of this has changed. Powerful competition from imports, greater cyclicality in the economy, and rapid technological change have forced firms to fundamentally reconsider the nature of their business. "Business as usual" is now a recipe for disaster. Consequently, the current tidal wave of corporate restructurings has occurred. Corporations are both acquiring and divesting at a record pace.

Open the newspaper to the financial pages and the issues jump out at you. The headlines are often larger than life, with sensational and dramatic qualities. For the average reader, most of the time they are distant and remote happenings, great news for the media, but rarely close to home. That is, until those same issues hit home when the same reader finds himself or herself on the receiving end of a major corporate reorganization.

Consider these examples of "ordinary" headlines that appeared in one two-week span:

¶ A West German publishing conglomerate announced agreements had been reached to acquire a large US book publisher, the name of which is recognizable to millions.

¶ One of the top supermarket chains in the western US agrees to merge with a large midwest chain, creating a new company that would rank near the top ten publicly held supermarket chains.

¶ A major West Coast bank, rumored in financial straights for more than one year, appears to be planning with another major western bank for one of the largest bank mergers in US history. Rumors are published of the beginning of "golden parachute" contracts for many top executives.

¶ One of America's top corporate raiders has offered a lucrative deal to purchase one of the country's oldest and largest steel companies.

¶ A small group of California investors plans to purchase one of the largest specialty ice cream retail chains from a major southwestern conglomerate. Upon that event, the controlling group will acquire yet another ice cream company.

The headlines range from books to supermarkets, banks to ice cream chains, and the desperate struggle for survival of the steel industry. The meshing of giant companies knows no limits. This book will show that somewhere within all this seeming corporate chaos, there are planned, rational business entities and beneficiaries. There are winners and there are losers. As we explore the sources and results of corporate chaos, we shall see how to identify the likely winners and how to best protect against becoming a loser.

EXECUTIVE SUMMARY

- Mergers and acquisitions are restructuring the corporate landscape in America.

- The human fallout from corporate restructuring can be devastating. *No one is safe*.

- The clever employee must adopt a personal strategy and a philosophy for survival in this era of economic turmoil.

ENDNOTE

1. Magnet, Myron, "Help! My Computer Has Just Been Taken Over," *Fortune*, 9 July 1984, p. 44.

2

THE TURF: BASIC CONCEPTS IN ORGANIZATIONAL DYNAMICS

There are different reasons for trying to fathom the complexities of an organization. One may be contemplating an investment, considering a career move, or sizing up a competitor. The task is made all the more difficult when one attempts to study organizations caught in the throes of a major restructuring. Of course, given unrestricted time and access, one could delve far below the surface to find the persons and places with the answers. How, then, with limited resources, can one begin to understand corporations undergoing such rapid change? How can one get right to the core of the matter? To understand the corporate chaos of today, and to survive it, there must be an effective way of penetrating the layers of bureaucracy, public relations, and secrecy. The following six concepts (intellectual hooks to hang ideas together) enable us to do just that and provide us with a sense of adventure along the way:

¶ Climate

¶ Culture

¶ Character

¶ The iceberg model

¶ Organizational core

¶ Image and salience

These are the six conceptual building blocks for analyzing organizations as they encounter change, restructuring, and trauma.

CORPORATE CLIMATE

The climate or "weather system" of an organization is a metaphorical reference to the state of company morale, as measured by surveys or objective interviews. Does the organization have a sunny, pleasurable climate, where morale is high and the people are happy and energized? Or is the climate turbulent and stormy, where morale is low and employees are discontented? Are meteorological conditions stable, or are there "seasons" corresponding to the corporate life cycle? Is there a long drought followed by a long, dark period?[1]

Climate is caused by a number of key forces, including leadership styles, type of industry, pay levels, and group perceptions about where the organization is headed. It can play a role in determining productivity and can make the difference between success and failure. If ignored, climate can lead to major problems.

When corporations are undergoing dramatic change, corporate climate can be the major indicator of how well the company is adapting. Mergers are like marriages. During the period after a merger, a brief honeymoon will occur while the two partners become more intimately acquainted. However, passion can give way to paranoia, and the climate can turn stormy. Employees will begin to wonder if they fit in with the new organization. Some will be asked to leave, others will be living on borrowed time. The ability to maintain healthy morale during this period is a key determinant of merger success. Corporate climate issues will be addressed as we explore the various sources of corporate chaos in the pages that follow.

CORPORATE CULTURE

Few concepts from the world of business and management have had such play in the popular press as corporate culture. In recent best sellers, its role has been touted as one of the major variables in the success formula.[2] A clear understanding of the behavior of an organization can be derived from careful observation of cultural phenomena. Therefore, when we study a corporation, it is just as important for us to observe the culture as it is when we tour a foreign country. A few key points about corporate culture need to be made.

Corporate culture is quite a simple concept. It means that an organization has its own norms, customs, roles, rituals, ceremonies, uniforms (or dress), and symbols. These are all essential building blocks of culture in any context. Organizations are really *minicultures* within societies and therefore embody many of the basic characteristics of larger or national cultures.

Every organization exhibits a culture that is specific and unique. This uniqueness relates to the nature of competition, the nature of the work itself, the nature of the owner's personality, and so on. For example, each corporation develops its own status symbols, which can be very important aspects of its culture. Understanding this *quality of uniqueness* is not an easy task; however, it should be one of the goals of a diagnostic exercise.[3] After examining specific details of organizational culture, we are able to develop greater insights into the next level of understanding: organizational *character*.[4] Understanding culture thus leads to understanding character.

CORPORATE CHARACTER

Psychologists have developed the concept of individual differences to explain personal identity. This is the notion that, despite the human characteristics that make us all similar at the most general level of personality, we are all unique individuals. Each of us is actually the sum of an infinite list of qualities and experiences that set us apart from others. The particular combination is so intricately different for each human being that any given expression of a particular experience or attitude is the tip of the iceberg, or a small subset of the total realm of experience. As we are all different in experience and outlook, so we all express our individual differences.

So, too, are organizations collections of individual lives and systems, exhibiting qualities of uniqueness. They are, in fact, constellations of highly complex information, made up of the lives of the people and things that are embodied within the boundaries of the corporation. Understanding such systems means that we must necessarily start to limit the information to an understandable level. We must start somewhere, so we begin with what we are given at the outset. An iceberg![5]

Organizational character is a concept that first appeared in the literature on organizational management. Chester Barnard said, "Organizations seem to have a life of their own." He used the phrase to suggest that organizations are not unlike individual human beings in the sense that they possess an inner belief system, individualistic behavior, and a unique identity; in fact, organizational character can be thought of as organizational "personality."[6] Every organization has a unique character (or personality) of its own. It is what individuals sense and talk about in very general terms. It is what employees "feel" after some time in an organization. And it is what keen diagnosticians are able to discern after brief experience in an organization. Just as a skilled clinical psychologist is able to accurately describe the personality of a new patient after only an hour's interaction, a skilled organizational diagnostician should be able to describe the organization's character and personality. This is not an area for "right or wrong" answers; it is an area for description and hypothesis formation.

THE ICEBERG MODEL AND THE ORGANIZATIONAL CORE

Corporations are like icebergs (see Figure 2.1). They are large, often very cold, frequently quite impersonal, and sometimes dangerous; most important, however, they are like icebergs in terms of their partial visibility (at least from a surface view).

There are four ranges to consider in observing icebergs. An analogous situation exists in diagnosing organizations.

1. The first range is that of *passerby data*. This means, simply, that which is visible, understandable, or perceivable by the casual observer. Nothing sophisticated, nothing complex; in fact, many viewers are not interested in going below the surface. However, the portion above the surface is a small part of the whole entity. Conclusions drawn from observing things above the surface are likely to be superficial and misleading. It is necessary to dive below the surface to reach a more meaningful level of understanding.

Figure 2.1   The Iceberg Model. A. Generic Iceberg Model. B. Iceberg Model Applied to Perception of Merger and Acquisition.

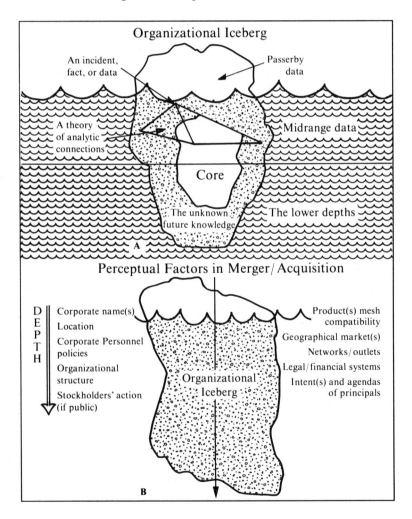

2. The second range is what is termed *midrange data.* This area is obtainable through conscious seeking, purposeful questioning, and the process we have called organizational diagnosis. One sees far more than the casual passerby does. In fact, there is far more to see below the surface, but it requires a greater motivation to see it. Frequently, important things are stumbled upon (see box) in this search, and the diagnostician can make some connections among various pieces of data. These connections help to form theories or understandings of the total organization and what "makes it tick." To understand the effects of corporate chaos, it is absolutely necessary to probe beneath the surface and collect midrange data.

Some would say it is not so accidental, but rather part of a commitment process. Goethe stated:

> Until one is committed, there is hesitancy, the chance to draw back, always ineffectiveness. Concerning all acts of initiative (and creation), there is one elementary truth the ignorance of which kills countless ideas and splendid plans: that moment one definitely commits oneself then Providence moves too. All sorts of things occur to help one that would never otherwise have occurred. A whole stream of events issues from the decision, raising in one's favor all manner of unforeseen

---

> incidents and meetings and material assistance, which no man could have dreamed would have come his way.
>
> Whatever you can do or dream you can, begin it. Boldness has genius, power and magic in it.
>
> Begin it now.
>
> —Goethe

3. There is a third range in icebergs that could be called the *lower depths*. This is an area almost never seen by human eyes, the implicit aspects of organizational culture. There are data and understandings that will rarely be obtained. One person could literally spend a lifetime studying a given organization, yet there would be no end to new understandings, perspectives, and information.

4. The most important region of the iceberg is the *core*. This concept will become crucially important in diagnosing corporations and what they may be about to do. Icebergs form around a core. Cores are the innermost ingredients or components of icebergs and are very difficult to reach. They can be quite small and represent a greater density of mass than the rest of the iceberg.

Organizational cores are similar to the core of an iceberg. They contain the difficult-to-reach, critically important seeds of organizational culture. They are the wellsprings from which the rest flows. They frequently are the simplest facts, yet they are the ones that remain hidden from the eye of the casual observer. They may number only two or three, but they may explain hundreds or thousands of other aspects in the organization's culture. They frequently relate, as with icebergs, to the earliest days of formation. They are at the center. They explain much of the existence of the organization. If altered or modified, vast changes in the rest of the organization are likely to ensue. It follows, then, that core issues are the decisive factors in merger success.

In our exploration of organizations experiencing cultural chaos, much of the adventure is in finding and diagnosing the organizational core. It is a difficult concept to grasp. Different experts may arrive at several different *core statements*. Nevertheless, large numbers of experts would probably agree upon a few central statements about a given organization as being the core variables or phenomena.

Core Details

It can be genuinely fun to look for "core" details and artifacts. Anyone can be Sherlock Holmes in pursuit of the secret clues! These are small "pieces" of evidence that are indicative of the essence. They are part of the "quintessence." Usually they are below the surface and appear to be secondary or trivial at first glance. Experienced consultants and experts know better! Their wisdom points to the small, sometimes unobtrusive, data and detail that can determine the destiny of a company.

Some years ago, we learned this the hard way. We were involved in consultation to small, rather low-tech industries struggling to survive. Originally hired on a management training mission, we soon realized that nothing, not even the best training programs delivered with top talent, enthusiasm, and sincerity, would fix the situation. The fact that the founder and CEO of one of the companies was a highly seasoned, functional alcoholic did not, at first, appear to be a serious problem. He seemed to be quite benign, providing the funds for training and staying out of the consultants' way.

Finally it became clearer. Nothing that could be done with, or for, the supervisors and managers could hide the fact that they were totally demoralized as a group, angered at the occasional tantrums the CEO would throw, and discouraged that the company and its leadership had deteriorated to its present level. Nothing could change that fact, and nearly all the company's *business* problems were a result of this man's one big problem—his unmanageable life and uncontrollable drinking. Finally the company was acquired, stripped of its assets, and many people lost jobs. Ironically, this small company had been one of the strongest in its industry and had had a very good asset position in its early, optimistic days. The slide lasted about 15 years. Astute consultants *could* have literally sniffed out the problem, *the core detail* for the company, in the earliest days. Eventually the son of the founder became a playboy and an alcoholic himself and sold the company for the father in the last days. The father, founder of one of New York State's top paper mills, is now in a hospital, dying of his disease.

An illustration is helpful at this point. If a small manufacturing organization is owned and managed by a family (father, son, brother-in-law, etc.), much of the organization's behavior will inevitably be influenced by this single core fact. It is almost impossible to render a thorough understanding and diagnosis of this organization without first understanding such an important reality. The fact that this particular organization exists on a particular acre of land in a particular town may not be a core fact, because such a fact alone does not necessarily determine observed organizational behavior. The family relationship, on the other hand, does influence behavior greatly.

Core Health and Core Pathology

The fact that patterns of corporate behavior are recognizable is just the beginning of the challenge for most of us. There are still other pitfalls awaiting us in this game. There is another big problem in trying to figure out what may be going on inside a company. This has to do with the *elusiveness* quality. And this relates intimately to sickness and health.

One unmistakable truth about human nature underlies all of what we have to say about this subject. Our strengths are our weaknesses. Our frailties are our virtues. It is only a matter of application, balance, and degree. We have often seen the case of the executive who pushes too hard. The same type A behavior and values that got the individual to the brink of success is the personality trait that pushes him over the line into a state of cardiac crisis or marital crisis. The same shyness that kept a genius out of the limelight in high school and teen life is the quality that enables the individual to withstand great stress later in life when career success begins to mount. The same ability for an individual to remain unattached to corporate life and pursue individualism to the point of great success as an entrepreneur is often the quality of detachment that prevents the person from leaping forward into meaningful relationships when it might help. The same core behavioral neurosis or pro-clivity expresses itself in different ways, in different modes of sickness or health, effectiveness or failure. The thing we are talking about here is a central feature of personality. When managed and disciplined, it sustains personal livelihood and career continuity. When the pendulum gets stuck or swings too far, the individual loses position, burns out, and may begin to hurt others and the corporation where he or she is employed.

Because the ultimate weakness that causes downfall, distress, and harm to others derives from the same *source* which produces the strength, it has the appearance of Jekyll and Hyde or just outright elusiveness. When executives go too far and do harmful things, it is often found that they had otherwise stellar careers and characters. The big mistakes appear to be out of context. "Bad" boys appear often to be "good" boys who strangely flipped out. The big names involved in 1986 insider trading were people who had impressed Wall Street analysts with their sheer brilliance and professional dazzle. In most of those cases, what could be considered in retrospect a latent blossoming of unbridled ego-mania had earlier taken a more acceptable form.

One vivid case illustrates the application of the iceberg model to understanding corporate chaos. In the mid-1970s in rural Illinois, a major electronics industry giant located a huge plant and manufacturing complex in the middle of the farm "Bible belt." At its head the company put a man, Noel, who was a southern gentleman at heart. He had grown up in rural Kentucky and had had a very traumatic childhood. He witnessed much tragedy in his immediate family, and at the age of 12, he cared for his younger siblings because his parents could not. By the age of 42, he had risen to division manager and became plant manager. For over eight years this individual ran a successful operation for the headquarters group, located in a large Eastern city. Noel used organization development consultants and team-building meetings to forge a highly loyal and close management team. Even with the rebellious union, Noel made sure that there was a real level of teamwork in the plant. He developed a program, for example, in which the union officers and the management team would identify some of the win-win things that could be done at the plant. Through the "uniman" (an acronym for "union and management teamwork") program, Noel's plant did marvelous and unusual things. Joint Christmas parties, charitable drives, sporting events, in-plant meetings, and safety improvements resulted. Division officials and senior corporate leaders from New York visited twice a year and always questioned Noel about these approaches. Yet nothing changed for the worse. Uniman programs went on for nearly six years, and teamwork and "family" feelings developed in this small, rural Illinois community. Noel had recreated his lost family. He stood for certain values—respect, extra-mile caring, team spirit, and the *complete absence of fighting.* Noel was truly a loved and respected man in his "family," and his plant fared well. It was like Camelot for a brief and shining few years.

But the family did not extend to New York. Nor Tokyo, for that matter. As Japanese competition heated up, Noel felt increased pressure, yet he kept the uniman and teamwork programs going. A new boss from New York took his first look at Noel and his efforts, and ordered the programs shut down. Unknown to Noel, the man also started to find his replacement. There was a fight, but Noel did not join in. The union struck, and management from New York responded by closing the plant for three weeks in the depths of the winter. Noel did not fight. He cared for his family, including the uniman people. He helped them as if they were younger siblings. His great caring and love never transformed to rage, let alone anger. And just as quickly as it all happened, Noel was transferred to a "sleepy hollow" facility four states away. A strong plant manager was brought in and lasted 13 months before the plant was shut down permanently. Fourteen hundred plant employees are now farming or doing other work in north-central Illinois.

What constituted Noel's great strength, his core-being, was, under changed circumstances, his unfortunate downfall in that company. Few analysts could have seen that coming! Yet it was all there. Personal experience and many hundreds of hours spent with Noel and his people before the fall did not produce the insight that is now so obvious. We see Noel and hear from him at Christmas every year. He found another company and still manages with loyalty, love, and a complete abstinence from hate and hostility, just as he did then. He and his own and his "company family" enjoy life now on the western slope of the Rockies, again in a small town, where it is once again possible for Noel and his spirit to be what he wants and apparently needs to be. For all the examples of subtle pain and pathological attributes of core-personhood that one sees in the very real profession of management counseling, the memories of Noel and his enduring values are enough to sustain one through the tough ones.

The Hidden Dimension

Sometimes the most important detail of the core is hidden from first glance. It can be very obscure or so seemingly simplistic that intelligent, astute analysts can miss it. Location is a good example. Companies located in isolated places frequently develop strange cultural phenomena that are difficult for outsiders to understand. A large New England pharmaceutical firm acquired a small biomedical electronics enterprise in the Florida panhandle region. Managers from the two companies just never got along. Transportation and communication difficulties arose and threatened to ruin the merger, which all experts in the industry predicted to be a sure bet. The Florida firm had never used private mail carriers or telefax machines, nor were there any fast delivery services located within range to service the fast parts delivery system that the Boston headquarters required. This small "detail" caused an unplanned expenditure of over $730,000, the cost of helicopter services, during the first year. No one had anticipated this expense in the preacquisition analysis. Getting the Florida plant personnel to accept the helicopter pad in the small community and getting the managers to use the service effectively were the second half of the problem. The town council passed "traffic regulations" and "curfew" hours that further jinxed the merger.

CORPORATE IMAGE AND SALIENCE

From extensive research on corporate image dynamics, two useful concepts emerge that can help to unravel the mysteries of corporate destiny—primary image and salience. These concepts enable us to collect useful information that we may bring to bear on the question of merger success or failure.

Each corporation has a distinct public image. The primary image is a fundamental set of commonly held views about the firm. The elements that compose this primary image are selected by the observer as the most conspicuous, or most salient, facts about an organization.

To return to our iceberg analogy, "first impression" or passerby data are the most salient. Midrange data are the next most salient. Hidden data, such as that found at the lower depths or the core, have no salience. Salience is also determined by the *einstellung* (mindset) of the observer. Facts that are salient in the context of a merger or acquisition decision may not be salient in the context of a marketing decision.

LIFE AFTER THE MERGER: COLLIDING CORPORATE CULTURES

A particular merger or acquisition is usually made for financial, marketing, or other strategic reasons, without consideration of organizational dynamics. Although, as we shall see in Chapter 4, nonrational motives may enter into the decision-making, research and experience have shown that matter-of-fact perspectives are powerful forces. After all, corporations do not mate for biological reasons. Strategic planning for mergers and acquisitions begins with the general question: Does the new business make sense? Then the questions raised by potential partners become quite specific: Are product lines compatible? Are synergies possible? Are geographic regions complementary? It is not surprising that the foundations of merger and acquisition strategies are rational business objectives. After all, most of the decision-makers who initiate the strategies and who eventually sign the merger agreements have climbed the corporate ladder through technical or functional disciplines, rather than risen through the ranks of human resource management.

After the merger, harsh realities of integrating the two organizations must be confronted. The business of corporate meshing is usually left as an afterthought to merger planning. The potential for corporate culture clash is rarely analyzed. These issues are placed on the back burner with the assumption that details will be worked out later. As a result, culture clash eventually emerges as a dominant issue. Problems of culture clash will not work themselves out if ignored. The integration of two disparate organizations must be actively managed, if the initial goals of synergy are to be realized.

Are corporate culture destinies appreciated in all of their dynamics by the founders of merger? Our research indicates that the leaders of corporate change do *not* appreciate the problems of implementing those changes. They are focused on the vision, the concept, the "ends," and the business motives for change.

Midlevel managers, however, *are* concerned about the process and are often able to relate to the business motives behind a merger. They are charged with implementation: Middle managers are given the job of making the concept a reality. These people are in the trenches; they must do the dirty work to make a merger successful. Very simply, they must learn to cope (see Appendix A).

For example, it may be the middle management staff that must be consolidated to create a streamlined corporation. This means that a manager of the division with redundant staff must now deal with firing decisions and the consequent drop in morale. But it was the architects of the merger—those removed from the day-to-day integration process—who authored the chaos in the first place. To the vast majority of participants, it was an edict from above that determined the destiny of the whole corporation. Sometimes we will hear an impassioned plea for help from these individuals. Sometimes they attempt to block the inevitable merger process, and this resistance leads to even further confusion. Why do they resist? Do they know something the founders and leaders don't know? Or is it simply a matter of resistance to change?

WINNERS AND LOSERS

For each of the cycles of corporate destiny, there is a definite set of winners and losers. Common sense reveals the harsh reality of corporate chaos: When two corporate cultures are joined, the stronger culture and players will ultimately prevail. Weaker ones will be dominated or eliminated. Who are the winners and losers? What are the typical patterns associated with each source of culture chaos? Can corporate character be preserved and shaped to maximize the number of winners?

HOW CLOSE TO HOME IT CAN BE

Behind the headlines of mergers and acquisitions are literally millions of people. Corporate chaos is fundamentally changing their lives. To illustrate the impact these issues can have on the quality of life of these people, consider the following example. Disaster and chaos could strike one family on multiple fronts. Rarely does it happen quite so dramatically as it did in the Ron Winston family.

Here is the cast of characters:

¶ Ron, the father, has been employed by a paper products manufacturer for 28 years in the Los Angeles area. He has just learned that his employer has been acquired by a large Chicago publishing company. Rumor has it that the Los Angeles unit will be phased down to accommodate a Japanese affiliate of the Chicago parent company. The Japanese company wants the unit to supply exclusive products for their new computer peripheral printer system. Ron is uncertain about a number of things. For one, he is uncomfortable about the new Japanese connection. He spent three years in active combat in the South Pacific during World War II, and his brother and cousin have been unemployed for six years in Flint, Michigan, as a result of the downturn in the American automobile markets worldwide. Additionally, Ron's whole pension program is rumored to be in jeopardy owing to litigation between the former employer and the program administrator. His current position is sales director, yet he is uncertain if the company will even be selling to existing markets. Fortunately, Ron's two children, Mike, now a doctoral candidate at Northwestern University, and Gretchen, recently graduated from Cornell's Hotel School, have finished college and most of Ron's payments have been made.

¶ Mary Winston, Ron's wife, has been an executive secretary to the head of a small ship repair company in the Long Beach area. After 14 years of service to the firm, her whole job is in turmoil. The employer just filed Chapter 7 of the federal bankruptcy code. This has meant a great deal of stress for her at work, plus the uncertainty of how much longer the job will continue. There are also rumors of a takeover by a larger competitor in the industry. Mary has had several unsolicited job offers from competitors, and her boss has been unclear about the future.

¶ Mike, the son, is writing a book based on his doctoral dissertation. A major publishing company (which happens to be a subsidiary of Ron's new employer) has tendered an offer to Mike for publishing rights to the new book, entitled *Video Journalism in Politics*.

The company has recently restructured its divisions, and Mike has just learned that the publishing area has been purchased by a conglomerate from Great Britain.

¶ Gretchen has an attractive offer from a major hotel chain. On her way to the interview in Philadelphia, she learns from headlines in the financial section of the *New York Times* that the chain is being bought by a major television network and film conglomerate. Rumors indicate that the hotel chain is part of the acquisition, but investment advisors are quoted as saying that the hotel business is being evaluated for sale to a French company. On the way to the interview, Gretchen learns that her airline ticket will not be honored by the airline owing to the announcement of a Chapter 11 status by the parent company. She holds in her hand the boarding pass printed by a machine made by her father's new employer.

The Winston family is an extreme case. Few of us are likely to experience the disruption that they did. But the phenomenon of corporate chaos is pervasive. Corporate life, for many of us, is filled with uncertainty. The vast majority of employees of large corporations are involved with the issues facing the Winston family—job security, relocation, and corporate identity. For most of us, these are the big issues, the survival and success-oriented aspects of corporate existence. Of course, there are many problems of a less critical nature—who the leaders of the company are, who the immediate boss is and what kind of personality he or she has, what working conditions are like, and so on. By virtue of their immediacy, they become the most important issues, but these job factors are determined by the larger patterns through which companies move. Our lives are being altered by basic changes in corporate strategies throughout the economy. All of us need to understand the patterns of change and how we can best survive. The next step in this journey is to learn about the key players and how they operate.

EXECUTIVE SUMMARY

It is necessary to see and understand corporate organizations as cultures and arenas where intricate games and human dynamics are played out. This chapter:

- Provides the basic concepts of culture, character, core, etc.

- Describes a method for understanding the uniqueness of a corporate culture

- Shows that the impact of corporate chaos can challenge traditional logic and wisdom about corporate behavior

We must look at corporations as we would icebergs from the cold deck of the *Titanic*—not with a sense of impending doom for certain, but with a sense of challenge and disbelief. We know full well how much we will never see below the surface. Yet, to navigate, we must anticipate and respect the depths of corporate entities. There are secrets worth investigating, and there are mysteries which, if detected, can spell the difference in surviving the trauma of corporate shock.

ENDNOTES

1. For an excellent discussion of organizational climate, using the meteorological metaphor, see Steele, Fritz and Jenks, Stephen, *The Feel of the Workplace* (Reading, Mass.: Addison-Wesley, 1977).
2. See Peters, Thomas and Waterman, Robert, Jr., *In Search of Excellence* (New York: Harper & Row, 1982).
3. A hallmark work on organizational diagnosis is Harry Levinson's *Organizational Diagnosis* (Cambridge, Mass.: Harvard University Press, 1972).
4. For an excellent discussion on the character concept, see William Wolf's *The Management of Personnel* (Belmont, Ca.: Wadsworth Publishing, 1961, pp. 9–25). Also, see Wright, Robert, *The Nature of Organizations* (Encino: Dickenson Publishing, 1977).
5. The "iceberg model" has become an effective conceptual model in organizational and management development work. Originally used by Stan Herman of TRW, and Wendell French and Cecil Bell more recently in *Organization Development: Behavioral Science Interventions for*

Organization Improvement (Englewood Cliffs, N.J.: Prentice Hall, 1984, p. 19) to show the more hidden, covert aspects of organizational life, it has become a widely used tool for looking more deeply at corporate cultures.

6. Barnard, Chester, *The Functions of the Executive* (Cambridge, Mass.: Harvard University Press, 1958).

3

EAGLES, PLANNERS, CULTURE CLUB: SCHOOLS OF THOUGHT ON CORPORATE CHAOS

Those in the executive suite or management firing line have a different perspective on the acquisition process from those who are once-removed as observers. Managers trying to make sense out of merger mania may get some insight by referring to the research and writings of external consultants and academics who analyze the happenings in the business world. (For this purpose, readers may wish to consult the references at the end of our text.)

The impact of merger and acquisition has indeed become a hot topic for contemporary business investigation. While residents of the "ivory tower" do not explain all of the resulting phenomena, they do provide a useful point of departure for studying contemporary corporate crises and chaos.

MOTIVES FROM PLACES ON HIGH

It should be made clear, lest any of our friends and colleagues misunderstand, that we identify with and relate to the motives of the writers and the theorists. In most cases, they are driven by altruism and the desire to provide useful knowledge to the planners and doers of the business world. Also, of course, they are interested in providing students with current, relevant grist for the mill of education—subjects worthy of study and intellectual analysis. Some academicians are also interested in the ethical dimensions of this activity, and they typically teach students about the gray areas of the law and how to examine insider deals, breaches of ethics, and corporate social responsibility.

We must also consider secondary motivations before looking at the evidence. In some cases, research is done for less admirable reasons. Bias may creep in when one attempts to substantiate a point of view (such as, "the US economy is suffering because of the numerous foreign acquisitions of American corporations"). Other research is done because there exists in many universities a subtle but strong "publish or perish" system. A relatively new area, such as corporate culture clash, may get a burst of attention because it is one of the ten or so hot topics on which little has thus far been done. Its importance or its researchability may be low, but it is very likely that for a period of time it will be a subject of research. These are the inevitable forces of motivation that constitute the path through which the merger phenomenon necessarily must pass, irrespective of whether or not the topic needs attention.

PROBLEMS IN RESEARCH

At least one of the forces limiting quality theoretical work on mergers is the difficulty inherent in the research of the topic. For example, in order to understand the motivations of top executives, one has to obtain extremely candid, penetrating interviews with individuals willing to be queried. This is extremely difficult for the academic. The alternative might be to examine motivation from a distance and to speculate on patterns of behavior. This approach is even less reliable since it really does not produce much from a scientific point of view.

Mergers are often sensitive, and it is difficult to discuss reasons and strategies because this may involve very personal and subjective motivations on the part of the raider. Wealth building is not something people like talking about! Likewise, the strategic motivations for an acquisition may entail competitive secrets that a senior manager would be reluctant to reveal.

Investigating the impact of mergers, we are dealing with one of the most complex processes of organizational behavior theory building. We are concerned with multiple causation, mutual causation, and unpredictability. Researchers like to consider cause and effect and statistical substantiation wherever possible. This is difficult to perform in looking at a force field of highly dynamic and nonrational organizational behavior. Perhaps the anthropological approach could be more useful. This usually involves the researcher immersing himself or herself in the culture as a participant–observer in order to study the patterns of behavior and culture change. Unfortunately, the process is lengthy and results in individual case studies—a method of research that is not in high regard among established theorists. They are more interested in studies that include large numbers of cases in the sample on which the analysis and conclusions are based. Identifying patterns in a given merger case is difficult enough, but it is not considered much of a contribution to the emerging theory. Yet, this is the methodology of the bulk of research on the topic thus far. Most of the studies reported are extracted analyses from broad reviews of cases in which the researcher was not present to view the culture impact.

SCHOOLS OF THOUGHT

In spite of the limitations, there is a growing and interesting body of literature. To organize it, we propose identifying three relatively distinct schools of thought: the "Professional Planners" school, the "Movers and Shakers" school, and the "Culture Club." Let's look at how each sees the world and the mergers and acquisitions within it. We beg the reader's indulgence: We have streamlined and simplified the complexity of each perspective in order to render it distinctive and memorable amid the chaos!

"Companies Are Numbers"

This motto derives from a school of thought best represented by the work produced by the leading management consulting firms. The main products were analytical tools for assessing the potential for corporate compatibility based on *product nature, market dynamics and structure,* and *key demographic data.* An economic assessment of merger potential constitutes the main strength of their approach. The implementation process was not really considered. The key tools were matrices for analytical corporate matchmaking. In the extreme case, buying a company is like buying products or x thousand shares of common stock on the New York Stock Exchange. Merging companies and the strategies that drive mergers become based on balance sheet logic. Will the consolidated balance sheets give a strategic advantage or new synergy ("one plus one equals three")?

Many of the brightest MBAs from the most prestigious graduate business schools fell into this number-crunching, data-base-driven mentality. Numbers and hard facts are, after all, what determine successful mergers and acquisitions! Interesting assumption, yet there is another one held by this school that makes the point even more clearly. All is reducible to a plan—if a merger is in the offing, a clear strategy is the prime need! This thinking, based on the notion of man as an economically motivated being, relies on rational models, sophisticated data analyses, and the existence of *a plan*. If it is remotely possible, a clever strategist can find a way. And a clever strategist absolutely needs a plan!

Humane considerations become secondary. Corporate culture is seen as some abstract and remote force, even an annoying concept introduced by the "soft" side of the house—the psychologists and anthropologists in the business schools. Most of the consultants advocating this type of planning are in the analysis business, not the implementation business. Most do not stay on for the program, but leave when the feasibility study is completed.

"Eagles Fly Alone"

The rallying cry for entrepreneurial pioneers has become "Eagles Fly Alone." Eagles are the top birds, at least in American culture, and flying alone has come to signify independence and solitary perseverance. Eagles must be sharp. They must survive the elements, go it alone, and rely on their own strength and keen vision. In fact, it has been our extensive work with entrepreneurs that has given us a deep appreciation of the eagle mentality. It deserves some explanation and focused appreciation. These are wonderful values when applied responsibly and need to be understood.

Many entrepreneurs fail several times to create viable businesses before they are successful. It often takes years of hard work and sacrifice. Some mortgage their houses and even lose their personal assets long before they attain wealth as successful business creators. Many of these individuals come from backgrounds that reward and reinforce the eagle mentality. As mentioned earlier, many are sons or daughters of entrepreneurs. The family tradition, its wealth and what it stands for, comes by hard-won accomplishments. Some have even overcome racial and ethnic discrimination through the years.

When the entrepreneur finally establishes a successful new business and accumulates wealth, the success and the business are sometimes managed carefully and very privately. Nothing is given away, including the right to direct and target new goals and marks of further success. This leads to one of the fundamental assumptions that applies to this school of thought: The entrepreneur and business leader (eagle) has the absolute right to make changes, govern corporate direction, and control corporate destiny, including acquisition and merger.

This supreme managerial prerogative is also expressed by the executives of major corporations.[1] Authors Mark Potts and Peter Behr describe this phenomenon in their recent book on executive leaders and corporate giants in the Fortune 100.[2] They portray their subjects as master craftsmen of corporate destiny, shaping their destiny scenarios with precision, molding their management style to fit the strategic plan, and then pursuing the objective fiercely. The implicit values are hard work, privacy, competitiveness, and prerogative. Gobble or be gobbled, raid or be raided, survive!

This school of thought is expressed in the path-breaking work of Michael Porter at Harvard and other theorists studying strategic management. Porter has written on the need for executives to manage companies for maximum competitive advantage by studying the driving economics of their industries. His work has been used enthusiastically by IBM and a host of other corporations seeking the competitive edge in the marketplace.

The work of Ian MacMillan of the Wharton School's Snider Center for Entrepreneurial Management also focuses on the eagle mentality. Other scholars have contributed to this growing body of literature on entrepreneurial management and strategy. Daryl Mitton's "The Compleat Entrepreneur" is a treatise on the behavior and astuteness that are both unique and essential qualities of the entrepreneur.[3]

What needs to be understood about eagles and this school of thought is this: Eagles are not inherently interested in people or corporate culture per se. It is the business reasons for merger and acquisition that prevail.

They are not uncaring about people. In fact, quite the contrary—they enjoy people. They are just driven by compelling business and personal goals.

They are likely to continue to run companies into the foreseeable future. Our best MBA and educational programs still prize the "spirit of the eagle," and the possibilities for personal accomplishment, given high motivation, remain outstanding.

Incidentally, eagles do not always fly alone. Occasionally, we find a dynamic duo or a small group of independent people who tightly craft a plan that has the same basic assumptions and values as solitary eagles have. They may fly with other eagles, but they never fly with turkeys!

The "Culture Club": Moderators or Players?

There are an estimated 50,000 people in the US alone who study and teach about organizational behavior. Many of these specialists have doctorates and some corporate consulting experience. A subset of these specialize in corporate culture, and a tiny subset (perhaps 50–100) are interested in merger impact on corporate culture. Only a handful have written about this fascinating topic, and we shall summarize their findings here.

What has been researched and what are the findings? A sample of key pieces of the mosaic:

1. Jemison and Sitkin have looked at the complexity of merger and acquisition processes. They have developed for further research a process perspective and model that relies on the notion of "organizational fit" and compatibility of components.[4]

2. Keith Halloran concludes that merger affects corporate identity in profound ways and relates this to culture changes in the new company after merger.[5]

3. Alex De Noble has studied the patterns and components of the postmerger integration process and has found several common themes relating to management applications, culture impact, and the human subsystem.[6]

4. Amy Sales and Philip Mirvis have studied corporate culture clashes and analyze their case studies through a conflict–resolution model.[7]

5. Gordon Walter has also studied cases in acquisition and merger and concluded that there are key areas for management attention and action in the transition process.[8] He has also looked at some of the critical dimensions of value conflicts in culture collisions.[9]

6. Howard Schwartz and Stan Davis zero in on the merger planning process and suggest specific strategy models for culture planning and compatibility issues.[10]

7. John Kitching, in a classic article in the *Harvard Business Review*, identifies some of the reasons why mergers succeed or fail based on "synergy scores." He suggests that the key issue is selecting the right people to manage change.[11]

8. W. Brooke Tunstall has studied the break-up of AT&T. He concludes that the culture change is the most profound challenge in the entire process. The important issue is to identify and retain the advantageous aspects of the culture during the transition.

Tunstall notes, however, that no model for this has been developed.[12]

PATTERNS?

Let's look at where the experts agree.

1. There is widespread agreement among the researchers that culture is affected by merger and acquisition. Ed Schein, Peter Frost, Ralph Kilmann, Stan Davis, John Kitching, Keith Halloran, David Jemison, Sim Sitkin, Gordon Walter, Philip Mirvis and Mitchell Marks, Alex De Noble, and others[13] discuss the impact on the acquired, or weaker partner.

2. The experts diverge on where the impact is most profound. Some have built models around a single explanatory variable. For example, Harry Trice and Jan Beyer suggest that we look at the central role of cultural rites and ceremonies in order to understand postmerger changes. Others have constructed more complex analyses involving several variables. For example, Stan Davis has developed a technique for assessing the cultural risk of marrying two organizations. This approach uses a matrix to measure cultural compatibility along the dimensions of values, norms, roles, etc. Alex De Noble and others have defined a process of "post merger integration" consisting of predictable stages and subprocesses.

Jemison and Sitkin have suggested that merger impact is felt in three main areas: administrative practices, personnel, and various "cultural" aspects. They identify specific parts of the process affecting the human side of the corporations: oversegmentation (breaking apart unit by unit) of the organization, escalating momentum (heightened psychological expectation), ambiguous expectations, and misapplications of management approaches to the merged culture.

This approach rests on the assumption that culture is a neglected but important "moderating variable." If managed well, cultural considerations could make the difference between a positive transition and a disastrous marriage. De Noble, for example, outlined four major categories where problems have occurred: reporting channels, control systems, information management, and systems management.

3. Most experts agree that there is increased stress following a merger or acquisition. Not all agree that this heightened tension leads to negative consequences. Mirvis and Marks conclude that there is an identifiable postmerger stage that they call "the merger syndrome." Halloran also talks about prevailing periods of social confusion after merger.

4. Although few of the theories extend beyond the immediate postmerger period, most experts would agree that the merger precipitates longer term, un-

planned consequences. It is perhaps also a result of the short term nature of merger–acquisition studies that few theorists have discussed any positive, synergistic effects.

5. A few theorists have dealt with the possibility of culture clash and what to do about it. Of the experts working in this field, most have used a reactive approach, attempting to introduce constructive healing, soothing remedies, and communication programs to jarred corporate cultures. A special few have had the rare opportunity to be proactive, bringing their expertise in early enough to mitigate problems. There is nearly a vacuum in the literature on this aspect thus far. Larry Williams has reported his early work with preventative approaches and the notion of "instant organization" as a strategy for proactive human resource-systems planning before and during mergers. One of the key variables in this limited area is the ability to work closely with the design team *early enough* in the process.

There would be a consensus, if one pooled the experts, that the process tends to be highly undermanaged by the executives in command. The corollary would be that the merged companies would be stronger if the process were approached in a proactive, considerate, planned way. When you query the experts, they often begin by saying, "There are a few good examples . . . ."

The Wave and the Gusher

It is interesting to note the images and analogies often used by "culture club" experts. They refer to the power of the process by using the image of a surfer riding a wave, or of an oil well that has become an uncontrollable gusher. The images suggest not powerlessness but respect for the phenomenon! And this brings us to the negative point that must be explored.

Academicians on rare occasions have the opportunity to significantly affect merger and acquisition cultures. Most often, when theoreticians get involved, they are in research roles, and it is not appropriate to do anything but describe what goes on. Very few individuals consult on strategies and make recommendations to the raiders and deal-makers themselves. It would thus be natural and logical for them to feel frustration, but few express it except to lament the lack of proper acculturation planning that surrounds merger activity. Some of the hardest bitten academicians have a feeling of contempt for the business leaders about whose companies they teach. And this is unfortunate. Especially when students pick up on their tone of disgust and despair.

Is the conclusion about near powerlessness and limited influence justified? Are the images of riding big waves and sitting atop powerful oil gushers useful? What does this say about the influence and contribution of the theoretical experts in one of America's most important socioeconomic eras—that of merger mania and the age of acquisition? Will the academic management community be able to make a meaningful contribution other than that of description and commentary?

THE IMPACT OF CORPORATE FUTURES

All along, we have known of the existence of movers and shakers and deal-makers operating alongside corporations. In our consulting cases, we have seen scores of situations where top management used the problem presented to the consultant as a shield so that the public and the rank and file would not suspect that the owners were setting the company up for an acquisition or a merger, or, worst of all, a planned Chapter 11 bankruptcy scenario. Thus, we need to ask, "What is really going on here?", not as a compulsive, paranoid knee-jerk to every event in organizational living, but in the spirit of enlightened self-interest. External consultants, academicians, and other professional researchers removed from the daily organizational fray may be in the best position, at times, to diagnose multilevel agendas in companies. Unfortunately, they are not installed in consulting positions at high enough levels either to confirm such possibilities or to influence the key players in their directives concerning corporate culture meshing.

There is more work to be done, clearly, in the theoretical and conceptual realm. We need to have more precise delineation of culture changes before and after merger. We need to know what the most sensitive pressure points are for management to utilize in strategic, responsible ways.

On the practical side, we would like to know more about successful and unsuccessful attempts to integrate or marry companies. The case literature is spotty. New vehicles and techniques need to be conceptualized and then tried out in acquisition scenarios. For example, noted systems theorist James B. Miller points out that there is not a mechanism or vehicle in corporate systems to allow for cultural blending or synthesis,[14] such as we see in a wide variety of examples in the natural sciences. There is just no guarantee that the acquired culture will retain any medium term coherence or traits in the new or dominant culture. Some would have us look at ways to preserve the positive elements, yet no vehicle exists to guarantee any form of retention.

Some state legislatures are moving toward concern for the environmental impact of merger activity. Under study are various forms of protective mechanisms to soften the harsh effects of merger–acquisition activity on local communities. Labor officials are increasingly challenging the more blatant impact issues, such as the appropriateness and the legality of golden parachutes for privileged executives. Rank and file employees usually get no such deals, nor are they even aware of the golden deals that their leaders are receiving.

The Realm of Ivory Tower Politics: Eagles Fly Where "Culture Clubbers" Fear to Tread?

On every business school faculty, there is a healthy dimension of scholarly competition and collegial rivalry. Sometimes it is so thick, however, that it leads to nearly total paralysis, and people literally do not talk to each other. In the teachings and in the arena of the "eagle school," and within the domains of the "planners" and the "culture club," we have the potential for such patterns of intellectual and collegial conflict, and we might have the potential for some interesting contribution and dialogue.

Basically, planners study possibilities, stay objective, and try to remain out of value debates. If a marriage is possible, they will find the right partner.

Culture clubbers primarily are engaged in a struggle for legitimacy and acknowledgment. They are naturally suspicious of "eagle school" mentality. Eagles and those academicians who champion their ways are seen as the people who make life difficult. They are viewed as a group of wealthy, compulsive achievers who are not interested as a whole in the human side of companies and the cultural field that has developed in the 1980s.

Conversely, eagles view culture clubbers as pedantic, abstract peddlers of irrelevant ideas. They are deplored as critics and as people to be avoided, with much the same tone that many politicians reserve for the press.[15]

IVORY TOWERS IN CHAOS?

Just like the reality of corporate America with its multiple constituencies and inevitable structure of heterogeneous agendas and interests, the world of theory and academic management is also a part of this larger mosaic of pluralistic society. It, too, has its kingdoms, fiefdoms, and movements. It, too, is part of corporate chaos. But this is not new to academics. A famous concept in management theory is Harold Koontz's notion of the "management theory jungle." Over two decades ago, he postulated that the world of information and those who teach about it and research it are expanding in the universe, yet this growth has not produced a language or theories that "talk to each other." And if the theories and methods don't talk to each other, how can the people who design the theories be expected to talk to each other either?

Each of the constituencies in the corporate world has an agenda. And each has a corresponding set of theorists whose work may be of interest. The following, for example, are the key players in the merger–acquisition arena:

¶ Owners and stockholders

¶ Stewards

¶ Raiders

¶ Brokers and investment bankers

¶ Managers

¶ Employees

¶ Unions

And within the world of academic management:

¶ "Professional Planners"

¶ "Eagles" and entrepreneurs

¶ "Culture Club"

The planners align their activities, interests, and agendas behind the owner-investors, the broker-bankers, and the managers when they are asked to perform their task of finding the ideal elements of a takeover scenario. Those in academia and the theory jungle who are interested in eagles work with owners and raiders but are wary of the brokers and the common manager. Elite eagle observers are not interested in employees and have mostly disgust for unions. And it is the stewards, managers, and employees who are interested in issues presented by the theorists of corporate culture. Occasionally we see an eagle who is interested in culture and the whole picture.[16]

EXECUTIVE SUMMARY

- The academic view of corporate restructuring must be understood in terms of competing disciplines.

- There are different schools of thought about merger and acquisition activity. Some hold entrepreneurs next to God, or at least as high as Jefferson and Lincoln! The classrooms and research are exciting and electric. A national cadre of seasoned entrepreneurs is emerging and returning to our classrooms in the best business schools.

- Other experts take a more scientific, detached approach—the school of rational deal analysis and professional corporate planning. These academicians hold that good planning, specifically business and financial planning, is the key.

- Behavioralists prefer to analyze and consult in terms of culture and clinical theories. Cheating, lying, and manipulating are rarely studied; the "good" qualities of "good" mergers are praised—leadership, teamwork, cooperation, etc. The pompous behavioralists hold contempt for many of the deal-makers, and the feeling is often returned with slurs about "ivory tower soft theory." Much is missed both ways.

- Ultimately, most of the academics hold different views, driven by disciplinary training and reinforced by the rewards of the professorial publish-or-perish system and internal university politics.

■ In fact, much of the actual research is inconclusive or self-serving. A broad mosaic of case studies and a few interesting autobiographies are beginning to emerge. We are far from a theory or a definitive conclusion about what is best for all. That may be very unlikely indeed.

ENDNOTES

1. Steven Jobs describes this spirit as a "pull from something out there" not a drive from within. For an interesting portrait of this spirit of independence and energy possessed by Jobs and several other entrepreneurs, see the 1986 PBS special, "Beyond Excellence."
2. Potts, Mark and Behr, Peter, *The Leading Edge* (New York: McGraw-Hill, 1987).
3. See Mitton, Daryl, "The Compleat Entrepreneur," a paper presented at the National Meeting of the Academy of Management, 1986.
4. Jemison, David and Sitkin, Sim, "Corporate Acquisitions: A Process Perspective," *Academy of Management Review*, Vol. 11, 1986, pp. 145–163.
5. Halloran, Keith, "The Impact of M&A Programs on Company Identity," *Mergers and Acquisitions*, Spring 1985, pp. 60–66.
6. De Noble, Alex, "Mergers and Acquisitions: An Analysis of the Post Merger Integration Process," a paper presented at the Fourth Annual Strategic Management Society Conference, October 1984.

7. Sales, Amy and Mirvis, Philip, "When Cultures Collide: Issues in Acquisition," in Kimberly, J. R. and Quinn, R. E. (Eds.), *Managing Organization Transitions* (Homewood, Ill.: Irwin, 1984), pp. 107–133.
8. Walter, Gordon, "Key Acquisition Integration Process for Four Strategic Orientations," Annual Meeting of the Academy of Management, 1985.
9. Walter, Gordon, "Culture Collisions in Merger and Acquisitions," in Frost, P. et al. (Eds.), *Organizational Culture* (Beverly Hills: Sage Publications, 1985), pp. 301–314.
10. Schwartz, Howard and Davis, Stanley, "Matching Corporate Culture and Business Strategy," *Organizational Dynamics*, Summer 1981, pp. 30–48.
11. Kitching, John, "Why Do Mergers Miscarry?" *Harvard Business Review*, November–December 1967, pp. 84–101.
12. W. Brooke Tunstall, "Cultural Transition at AT&T," *Sloan Management Review*, Fall 1983, pp. 15–26.
13. See Reference section for specific references of these authors.
14. Miller, James B., *Living Systems* (New York: McGraw-Hill, 1978).
15. We have developed these characterizations, first, because they are real and *point in the direction* of actual social interactions and "turf" issues within the establishment of academic management. Also, to help clarify the complexity of the various "kingdoms" within academia.
16. Peters and Waterman, and their subsequent PBS television specials, have featured some of these masters of multiple worlds. Most memorable is the vignette depicting the owner-entrepreneur who makes awards to common folks for uncommon valor in the trenches of everyday

work. He talked emotionally about his love for the people and broke down in tears when reflecting upon their qualities. We might view him as an eagle with a warm heart.

4

THE PLAYERS AND
THE ARENAS

There are many communities of interest whose lives and bank accounts are affected by the cycles of corporate destiny—unions, stockholders, investment bankers, arbitrageurs, and corporate raiders. Some have reaped enormous benefits, others have sustained losses, but none have emerged untouched by the forces of growth, adaptation, and decline. In this chapter, we shall examine the major players—from victorious to vanquished, from king to pawn—and the arenas in which they joust.

UNIONS: HERE TODAY, GONE TOMORROW

Union-busting is a major corporate strategy designed to free owners and managers from an association they deem destructive to the interests of the firm.

Consider the case of a large, well-known air carrier, which first underwent a crippling strike, then a voluntary bankruptcy, and finally a major reorganization. Now, some two years after its reorganization, the airline is back in a sound financial position, delivering profits to stockholders and providing thousands with jobs in the once disaster-stricken airline industry. Although this seems an unqualified success, not everyone emerged victorious—the union that once was is no longer.

Several large retail chains, historically union hotbeds in the western United States, have also reorganized in an attempt to shake off labor's powerful grip. For example, over a two-year period, a large retail chain changed its name, gave all its stores a physical overhaul in layout and appearance, and reoriented its business to a more wholesale price/quantity market. Former employees were fired, the union disbanded, and the company reorganized without the union within 12 months.

CORPORATE RAIDERS: FOLK HEROES OR ZEALOTS?

Another key player in the great merger game is the takeover artist, a.k.a. the corporate raider. Members of this group, which include such diverse personalities as Irwin Jacobs, Carl Icahn, Frank Lorenzo, Sanford Sigoloff, Donald Trump, Meshulam Riklis, and T. Boone Pickens, have been catapulted to national prominence as the great folk heroes of modern financial times. Their backgrounds and areas of expertise differ widely. Some come from oil and real estate, others from high tech and transportation. Some were born in rural Texas, others hail from Manhattan. How can we hope to understand such outwardly dissimilar individuals, to comprehend their personal and practical reasons for acting the way they do, to learn how to work with their sometimes unpredictable styles? Although each has a unique life story, we can discern a set of common themes and motivations.

One common theme appears to be the need to develop a corporate father–son relationship, either to replace a kinship that used to be or to create a bond that never was. Some raiders had fathers who were either shining examples of success or were financial disasters. Others were orphans or had parents who left them early in their lives through family misfortune or death. Most takeover artists recreate the lost family within their companies either by fostering a small, tightly bound group of corporate loyalists or by building a cabal within "secret places" in their empires or subsidiaries.[1] Some even sponsor ("father") others within their companies or find surrogate fathers of their own. One of the authors consulted with a raider who was in his mid-forties and still sought guidance from a father–mentor in the community. When the elder man died suddenly, the raider felt a profound sense of loss and bewilderment. Fifteen months later, he realized how deeply he had tried to please and receive approval from the man. His activities and aspirations were confused for five years until he transferred to another secret role model across the country.

Another central theme in the raiders we have studied is their tendency to be mavericks. Most of them abhor corporate bureaucracy and run their own teams, selecting members who show fierce loyalty. They detest all the qualities that bring down great companies and stifle creativity, yet, ironically, they are only able to flavor their organizations to their own antibureaucratic liking to a limited degree.

WHOEVER HAS THE MOST TOYS WINS

The chief motivation in the *early* careers of the takeover artists is the acquisitive need *par excellence*. This typically involves the building of corporate empires—elaborate configurations of structure and corporate complexity. The object of the game is to accumulate personal assets, wealth, and an appropriate dose of status, usually in the form of a title and the trappings of office, e.g., automobiles, chauffeurs, executive staff and suites, etc.

Interestingly, later in their careers, these corporate empire kings undergo a shift of values and emphasis. It seems they attain a level of wealth beyond which the accumulation of more riches is no longer the primary goal. As basic financial security (or wealth) is virtually assured, attention can be turned to the finer causes and issues that exist within the newly formed financial empire.[2]

The literature is full of cases in which newly successful chief executives turn the page, concentrating more on pet projects and less on personal profits. Although the causes they choose to champion are often centered on themes of corporate growth, crusaders may also focus on internal themes, such as product quality, employee involvement, and personal excellence.[3]

One memorable case involved an executive who became obsessed with "tuning" his whole corporate structure. A weekend with his spouse at a sensitivity group retreat, sponsored by his church, became a veritable crusade. He returned from the retreat and invested his renewed energy, both psychic and emotional, in an organizational renewal process. The training function was elevated to new heights within the corporate structure. The chief executive became the leader of a personal-growth-centered program (not unlike the church weekend retreat) for all 300 top executives of the various companies he owned.

We don't yet know why we consistently see this progression from empire building to crusading. Perhaps we have an example of the famous Maslow hierarchy of needs at work in the lives of takeover artists. And there certainly are other frameworks for explanation of the pattern. Perhaps there is a terse *script*, a subconscious self-promise that reads, "I will never allow myself or my people to surrender their integrity for the sake of _____." Or, "I will not allow myself to return to the fear that I felt when _____." Such promises are strong, forming the keystones of many empires and the fortunes of those who build them.

It is also not surprising that the behavior exhibited in the business environment is by no means restricted to that milieu. These same motivational forces are manifested in other areas of the life of the executive—family, clubs, and charitable contributions. Personal tenacity is still there, whether it is exhibited in the boardroom or at the golf course.

BROKERS AND BANKERS: PROFESSIONALS OR CASINO AGENTS?

The frenzied merger and acquisition activity of the last decade has lined the pockets of yet another group of financial wizards—brokers and investment bankers. In a much-heralded piece in the *Atlantic Monthly*, writer James Fallows poses a central challenge to the financial community. In an era that has witnessed the rise of the "Casino Economy," Fallows alleges that the best and brightest from our public schools and private educational systems are heading into professions that specialize in reshuffling the economic deck through deal-making and elaborate strategies of business servicing rather than joining sectors of the economy that produce real increases in GNP. Fallows notes the irony of this trend:

> The perversity of such a preference is that students are hoping to find security in the very pursuits that add such instability to the American financial structure. This fall, *Business Week* featured a report on the "Casino Economy"—the tremendous increase in speculation, merger, corporate rearrangement, tax avoid-

ance, and other forms of financial churning that make fortunes for investment bankers while ratcheting up the level of corporate debt. To such efforts are the best and brightest now drawn.[4]

Who does the churning? Who are the deal-makers? Are they professionals or casino gamblers? Whatever the true nature of their character, one fact remains: These players are the controllers. These individuals hold the cards and, as a result, have developed, more than anyone else in the investing arena, a strong network of loyal parties, servicing agents, and a keen sense of directions in the market. In addition, they hold the power and the voting blocks of stock to move the market several points with one put or call.

ARBITRAGEURS: IT'S ALL JUST SPECULATION

Another gambler of sorts that has recently received an enormous amount of (adverse) publicity is the arbitrageur. Arbitrage experts buy bills of exchange, stocks, etc., in one market and attempt to sell them at a profit in another market. Most develop their expertise and make their fortunes in a particular market. For example, foreign currency specialists can make millions of dollars in a matter of hours following the ebb and flow of the international currency game. Although this high-stakes crapshoot is not for the fainthearted, arbitrage is a perfectly legal activity; in principle, speculators rely upon their instincts and intimate knowledge of their markets to make the correct moves and anticipate the trends.

INSIDERS: GO TELL IT ON THE MOUNTAIN

Insiders are those who are able to act upon information that is not generally available to the public. Inside trading on the stock market often involves third parties or surrogates[5]; the actual trading parties may be acting on behalf of others behind the scenes. Consider the typical inside deal:

> A chief financial officer for a major western airline has set up an elaborate system of inside trading with a business partner who buys stock in the airline one week before a merger with another airline. The chief financial officer knew the merger was close and was betting on the stock price rising the customary 15 to 30 per cent overnight. The business partner invested $200,000 on the New York Stock Exchange. The proceeds from the actual transaction netted the pair $42,000, and the balances were transferred to personal accounts maintained in a bank in the Cayman Islands. Later the monies were transferred to an account in a bank in Panama, and were withdrawn in cash during a vacation by both partners and their spouses.

In this case, the insider and the agent profited personally on the "merger market." In many such instances, the parties shield their activities with elaborate layers of disguise. The more complexity there actually is, the more remote the possibility of being caught.

Who are the insiders? What constitutes "guilty knowledge"? These questions have been examined by courts and critics and the answer is not altogether clear. It is best to say that the events of the mid-eighties will forge clearer answers for years to come. For a discussion of how the SEC is trying to police the problem, see the story in the box.

WHAT DID THEY KNOW—AND HOW?

Remember the late Supreme Court Justice Potter Stewart's definition of pornography? "I know it when I see it." If only recognizing insider trading were so simple. No federal law addresses it specifically. Existing definitions rest on Securities and Exchange Commission rules and a series of contradictory rulings. The result: A great zone of ambiguity.

It's clear from case law that a director who buys his company's shares knowing that a takeover bid is imminent is trading on inside dope. But someone who buys stock after overhearing a couple of loose-tongued corporate officers discuss an upcoming merger may or may not be doing so illegally—it might depend on whether the eavesdropper knew the executives' identities. What if your employer invents a device that makes widgets obsolete and you sell short the stock of Widget Industries? That's another murky area.

What is not disputed is that the SEC under Chairman John Shad has aggressively expanded the definition of insider trading. In recent years, the SEC has left few job titles and social classes immune from its crusade, nabbing big-time speculators and secretaries, cabbies and lawyers, investment bankers and journalists. Among the more prominent investors the SEC has tangled with are Paul Thayer, a former deputy secretary of defense and onetime chairman of LTV Corporation who pleaded guilty to obstruction of justice, and Thomas Reed, a former Reagan National Security Council staffer who was acquitted of criminal charges but agreed in civil action to repay $427,000 in trading profits.

Traditionally, an inside trader was one who bought or sold securities while possessing material nonpublic information—data capable of moving a company's stock price. Someone having such knowledge had to disclose it or abstain from trading, a doctrine that won judicial sanction in a 1968 appeals-court ruling involving executives at Texas Gulf Sulphur who had used word of a Canadian ore strike to reap stock profits.

But two Supreme Court decisions in the early 1980s narrowed the definition by requiring that the violator not only act on material information but also breach a duty or confidence. In one case, the Court overturned the conviction of Vincent Chiarella, a printer with access to tender-offer prospectuses before takeovers became public. The Court held that, since Chiarella was not a corporate insider, he had no fiduciary duty and was not obliged to notify those who sold him securities. In the other case, the Court reversed the SEC's censure of analyst Raymond Dirks, who alerted his clients to a massive fraud at Equity Funding of America before the scandal broke. The Court declared that the tipster who first warned Dirks had not breached his duty to Equity shareholders because he disclosed the information to expose fraud, not for profit. And since the insider didn't violate his fiduciary obligations, the Court added, neither did Dirks.

Yet SEC lawyers found elements in both *Chiarella* and *Dirks* that let the agency widen its net. The key language came in a dissent by then Chief Justice Warren Burger in the *Chiarella* ruling that encouraged the SEC to introduce a new "misappropriation" theory of insider trading. The theory holds that someone who trades on confidential information obtained from an employer has misappropriated it and could be violating securities law. "The SEC has used this theory very effectively," says Herbert Milstein, a Washington, D.C., attorney and former SEC enforcement officer. "In effect, they say in these cases that the insider has stolen information."

A series of decisions since *Chiarella* have upheld the validity of the misappropriation charge. In the most important ruling, a federal appeals court let stand criminal indictments against five people, including two young investment bankers, Adrian Antoniu and E. Jacques Courtois, who had worked for Morgan Stanley. The court said that someone in a position of trust who misused private data from an investment-banking firm could be liable under securities law. The same theory figured in the case of Kenneth Petricig, a former proofreader at a big New York law firm who fed inside information on takeovers to cabdriver Stephen Wallis.

In the most controversial application of the misappropriation theory, a federal appeals court last May upheld the conviction of former *Wall Street Journal* reporter R. Foster Winans for selling tips on upcoming "Heard on the Street" columns to a New York stockbroker for a share of the trading profits. Prosecutors charged that leaking of unpublished columns to traders constituted a theft of confidential information and a fraud against the *Journal*. But Alan Bromberg, a law professor at Southern Methodist University, is skeptical about the misappropriation theory's application to Winan's actions. Winans may have violated an employment contract or revealed trade secrets, Bromberg says, but it's hard to make the case that he violated securities law.

Ultimately, the Justices may review the misappropriation theory, perhaps in the Winans case. Bromberg, for one, thinks they will uphold his conviction. But what's really significant, Bromberg believes, is that a ruling on a Winans appeal "will give the Court a way to patch up the mess it made when it decided the *Dirks* and *Chiarella* cases."

SOURCE: Copyright, 1986, U.S. News & World Report. Reprinted from issue of Dec. 1, 1986.

STEWARDS

Another key player is the steward. As the term suggests, these individuals are entrusted with the destiny of the corporation. Formal vesting of power can be through conferment of title—board member, executive officer, senior consultant. A steward is a highly trusted player who is expected to act according to the interests of the corporation. These individuals have a fiduciary relationship to the corporate body and, as such, are bound to it in a role of high trust.

Stewards are often privy to information and knowledge surrounding merger and acquisition activity because they are asked for advice about policy decisions. Sometimes they are given the innermost, core intelligence about who is strong and who is weak, who will remain after the merger and who will be looking for employment. Guardians of precious inside information, stewards are expected to use it not for their own benefit, but rather for the good of the corporate entity.

STOCKHOLDERS (STAKEHOLDERS?)

The final major category of player is the stockholder. Stockholders have invested, individually or institutionally, in the destiny of the corporation. They are remote, yet their power and presence can be focused like the light of a laser beam. They can be passive and oblivious to the major forces affecting their chosen company, or they can wield amazing influence. That influence, exerted through sizable blocks of stock ownership, can cripple a company's decision-making processes or can be used to aid raiders. If an outside raider convinces a group of stockholders that their investment interests are better served by an acquisition scenario, these owners can move overnight to oust senior executives from their positions at the helm. For example, Carl Icahn brought a breath of fresh air to many beleaguered stockholders of USX (formerly US Steel). And in late 1986, Ross Perot traded his firm for large blocks of GM stock, using his newly acquired influence to challenge General Motors' senior management.[6]

When the players activate their agendas, they do so within discrete settings or "arenas." These may be professional communities with highly defined and codified standards, or "grey areas" that have little or no definition. They are the physical places and professional settings in which the players are found. In any case, players need arenas as places in which to play out their roles and seek rewards, and they need the audiences within those arenas to provide the all-important approval that is often itself the biggest reward.

Unions are mentioned as players in the larger game of corporate chaos. They play for big stakes—their very survival and existence in certain sectors of the economy and in companies in which they have had long, historical footholds. When they win in the decertification game, they win only temporarily, for they can be challenged again at the next juncture in union–management relations. When they lose, they typically lose for a specific bargaining unit the right to represent the employees for an indefinite future. Henceforth, the union no longer exists. The election becomes the point of sudden departure!

The arena itself in this sphere is the company setting, and the industry in which the union might have a significant role. Physically, the arena can be the company boundaries, but the players, the union leaders, the management staff, arbitrators, mediators, and the all-important specialists, the union-busting consultants, may conduct the game and the discussions over a large segment of corporate and geographical turf. These processes typically take place in low-profile meetings held in hotels, clubs, and even distant cities. Of course, the actual elections take place nearby or upon company property or within union halls. But the professional arenas are wide indeed. They include the realm of the legal profession, consulting experts, professional arbitrators, academic experts, union professionals, and the local leaders. Wherever they do business and operate is the larger arena of this activity.

Several years ago, one of the authors had the distinct pleasure(?) of meeting one of this country's most notorious union-busters. The meeting and the setting were absolutely uncanny. A third party referred the author to the individual who was located in a rather seedy section of suburban Los Angeles. It was difficult to find the location amid warehouses and truck loading areas in this vast concrete landscape. The building was a run-down warehouse with an outdated company name on the front. After entering the only entrance where there was activity or any life, a rear loading dock door, the author wandered through several layers of outer offices. On the way through the building, it became evident that this was indeed a very busy place! There were several hundred illegal aliens working at sewing machines making small textile products. The individual the author had been referred to was soon introduced, and we sat down for the auspicious conversational beginnings.

Within several minutes, we discovered that we were actually classmates from the same graduating class of a large Eastern university; in fact, we had the same major, and we reminisced about the same great old professors in our major—labor-management relations. He had spent several years as a torpedo expert with the Navy during the Vietnam era and began his industrial career as a field rep for one of America's largest, toughest unions in the Midwest. He rose through the ranks and became one of the most skilled union organizers and strategists, and all without a law degree. When asked if he had trained in law school, he grinned and held up one green book, a hardcover text on the details of labor law in the United States. "This," he said wryly, "was my legal education!"

His story was amazing, yet the result was chilling. Successful as a union organizer, he turned his collar over and became a consultant overnight for management of several companies he had penetrated as an organizer.

After his initial foray into the sobering occupation, he related that he ran a streak of ninety-three straight decertification elections that he had personally designed and orchestrated over a span of six years. Several of these, he was proud to say, were victories over Caesar Chavez in the fields and vineyards of California's agriculture industry. These "victories," he maintained, were the pinnacle of his career.

The man was still young, quite wealthy, and now serving as the president of a small, modest, and rather illegal textile product firm in backstreet USA. Why? What had removed him from his amazingly successful career?

Soon, he introduced his charming wife and two very young and playful children. They had come by the office to say "hello" and play with a pet bird, caged in the outer office. Pictures of the children surrounded the other framed "victory" letters attesting to NLRB election results, and a plastic model submarine, vintage Vietnam War era.

It was all so clear. Name change? Identity change? Strangely not. Was it that he still liked that small element of living dangerously, though he maintained a new lifestyle? Perhaps, though we can only surmise the real nature of the danger he faced from uncounted generations and numbers of faceless union friends. He admitted to a low-profile existence, though it surely provided him with all manner of material wealth. A lonely office in a lost suburb of a large city.

We have not heard from him now for several years, and we shall not soon forget the pauses in the conversation, the mosaic of trophies and photos on the wall, the voices of the children visiting their father at work that morning. We never knew each other at the university where we had taken the same classes, yet how little we knew then of the fascinating and complex and different paths that would bring us to a meeting twenty years later.

The corporate raiders, in contrast to union busters, operate in large and very public arenas. Their sphere of influence reaches into the world of banking, international finance, and corporate structures, as well as local small business areas, and they are often in the arena of the public spotlight. In fact, their world and turf is so large, their contacts so far reaching, that it boggles the mind. They buy blocks of stock and have intimate connections on Wall Street. They reach out for financial packages, so they have friends among the experts in the financial markets and brokerages. They deal with specific technologies, so they have their sources and private experts there. And they ultimately deal with the press, so they have a marketing or public relations resource somewhere! But their efforts are mostly directed at acquiring and merging specific corporations, so, in a sense, the raider's world eventually becomes manifest and reaches its sharpest focus in a specific company that becomes a target for a deal. The raider's larger arena finally becomes totally focused, and his influence when the "homework" has been done correctly can be powerful. The arena for a deal might become as small, as focused, and as vulnerable as a private boardroom luncheon with the target company owner, who, in his formal corporate role, is partaking of his last supper!

Brokers, bankers, and arbitrageurs live in a very specific and an increasingly technical world. Their arenas in deal-making are Wall Street and the stock market professionals, the world of commercial investment banking, and technical markets where information must be highly reliable, confidential, and technical. There are also private channels and special, personal relationships, perhaps "old-boy" linkages that involve old college friendships, war buddies, and other kindred spirits born of deal-making. Sometimes these lines of connection span vast networks of professional communities with global proportions.

Inside deal-making must rely on these relationships that are of the highest degree of confidentiality and mutuality. In analyzing these special networks, one can often discover their intricate nature of opportunism. It becomes a pact. If broken, one's professional world can crumble. Deals can go sour, yet the special networks must remain secure. There is great pressure to remain silent for fear of exposure, prosecution, and long-term professional isolation and castigation. Thus the "arena" is intricate and highly volatile. One is either "in" or an outcast. And the network, if you could diagram it, would be as intricate and as delicate as a spider's web.

Stewards who are board members operate in a double arena, with, theoretically, a single standard of morality. They must serve both privately and publicly, maintaining confidentiality and loyalty to stockholders and management at the same time. They can be asked to hold privileged information concerning impending merger and acquisition, yet they are expected to walk a very straight line and not use the information for personal advantage or to violate any loyalty, real or abstract, to the corporate leadership and its philosophical premises. As you might imagine, it is often a matter of interpretation and judgment. Conflicts abound. And when they crash down upon a board member or steward-consultant, the conflicts must be handled with discretion and dignity, privately and within the confines of the executive suite and inner sanctum. But the pressures are often public ones. It is in the public arena that the board member or corporate spokesperson must respond to hot questions and challenges.

Thus stewards must possess both private and public skills for the arena dynamics they will face. They require astute personal skills at politics and personal diplomacy for the internal world, and the deft poise and alacrity of a public orator or problem-solver for the outside. The arenas are different, though the pressures are equally trying.

And stockholders mostly operate in one big, distant arena—that of passive spectatorship in the big game of watching the fate of the company rise or fall. For the majority, this means truly passive behavior: occasional tracking of corporate performance; infrequent reading of the company proxy statement; less frequent voting or correspondence with corporate officials. Very few individuals ever attend annual meetings. Occasionally someone will adopt a cause, rally others, and attempt to wield influence. And most frequently when it occurs, it concerns a political, ecological, or technical issue. Rarely does it grapple with matters that really govern corporate destiny.

DIFFERENT STROKES FOR DIFFERENT FOLKS

Perspectives differ. They come from the unique interests and agendas of each set of players, and all mesh and mix to further create and reinforce the pattern of corporate chaos that we see on our greater corporate landscape today. Having identified the players and what we think may be their main interests and agendas, we may find it easier to sort out some of the music from the noise.

As we have seen, some of the players are playing specific games. They are out to win, and win big. Others, however, are out to do reasonably well or just survive. But we all have different places in the arena. We do not have equal influence. On the one hand, the raiders have great power. They have sweeping agendas and the wherewithal to accomplish them. On the other hand, many of us are small investors. We study the moves. We attempt to discern what is happening and which way to play our limited resources. The reality is that some players have a better starting lineup, and some are destined not to win at all.

Before dealing with the implications for most players, we need to understand more about the agendas of winners. Corporate empire building is the biggest one and, to some, the only game in town.

EXECUTIVE SUMMARY

- This chapter identifies some of those who are interested in merger and acquisition activity and some of the motivation behind each perspective. It is important to understand that there is not a neat convergence of economic or political interests here, much, in fact, to the contrary.

- Some are *direct* players in the game. They play with their personal wealth and fortune, and the stakes are large. Some lose everything—jobs, homes, even health and life itself.

ENDNOTES

1. The reason for the secrecy is that intimacy, though a driving human force within many communities, even the sometimes all-male executive family culture, must be

protected. The business intimates of the leader cannot afford to be seen publicly. The mystique of remote, objective leadership is maintained, and potential vulnerabilities are shielded.

2. See Risen, James, "Perot Says He Fought GM Officer Bonuses," *Los Angeles Times*, 9 December 1986, CC/IV.

3. The Peters and Waterman book, *In Search of Excellence*, became a tangible rallying point for many. See the appendix of Peters' recent book with Austin, *A Passion for Excellence* (Random House, New York, 1985), p. 421.

4. Fallows, James, "The Case against Credentialism," *The Atlantic Monthly*, December 1985, p. 51.

5. Furlong, T., Harris, K., and Delugach, A., "Anatomy of a Scandal: How Alleged Insider Trading Operated," *Los Angeles Times,* 14 February 1987. Also, Hiltzik, Michael, "Why Boesky Insider Trading Case Rocked Wall St.," *Los Angeles Times*, December 1986, CC/IV.

6. See "Trouble at GM: Angry Investors, Big Losses," *San Diego Tribune*, 18 December 1986, p. AA–1.

5

THE HOW AND WHY OF EMPIRE BUILDING

The statistics on empire building in the United States are overwhelming. *Empire building* refers to the entire range of activities designed to enlarge the size and power of the modern corporation and its managers. These activities include mergers, acquisitions (both hostile and friendly), leveraged buyouts, initial public offerings, joint ventures, and international investment. Many of these tactics are at their highest levels in history. A relatively strong economy, low inflation and interest rates, and creative financing have all combined to make these strategies available to even small firms and individual managers.

RESHUFFLING THE DECK

As a result of the tidal wave of mergers and acquisitions, the US corporate world is sailing into uncharted waters.

The intensity of empire building is striking for both its breadth and depth. Deal-making is an honored tradition on Wall Street. But even Wall Street has never seen anything like the activity of the early 1980s. The number of mergers, acquisitions, and joint ventures has reached unprecedented levels. Furthermore, in addition to a record number of deals, the size of the transactions is equally spectacular. The eighties have become the era of the billion dollar takeover. No firm—no matter how large—is safe from attack. During the period from 1983 to 1986, approximately 12,200 companies and divisions worth $490 billion have changed hands. This represents roughly 20% of the value of all securities traded in the stock market. According to *Business Week*, if such a pace were to continue through the year 2001, every public company in the United States would be under new ownership.[1] Figure 5.1 shows the phenomenal growth in mergers and acquisitions from 1980 to 1986. During this period, acquisitions grew at a compound annual rate of over 31% per year.

The large number of participating firms is matched by the enormous size of the players. As shown in Table 5.1, the firms acquired in 1986 are among the largest in the world: Beatrice, RCA, and Sperry were three of the biggest to be put on the block. Bank of America and USX (once America's largest bank and steel companies, respectively) spent most of the year worrying about hostile takeovers. *No one is safe.*

Figure 5.1 US Mergers and Acquisitions.

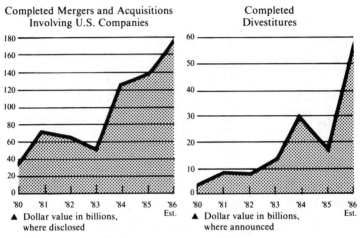

Completed Mergers and Acquisitions Involving U.S. Companies

▲ Dollar value in billions, where disclosed

Completed Divestitures

▲ Dollar value in billions, where announced

Foreign Purchases of U.S. Companies

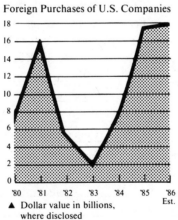

▲ Dollar value in billions, where disclosed

DATA: *Mergers & Acquisitions* magazine

SOURCE: Reprinted from January 12, 1987 issue of *Business Week* by special permission, copyright © 1987 by McGraw-Hill, Inc.

Table 5.1 The Billion-Dollar Deals of 1986.

Company	Type of deal	Buyer	Amount (billions of dollars)
LBO= LEVERAGED BUYOUT			ACQ.= ACQUISITION
	RECAP.= RECAPITALIZATION		
IPO= INITIAL PUBLIC OFFERING			JV= JOINT VENTURE
BEATRICE	LBO	Kohlberg Kravis Roberts	$6.3
RCA	ACQ.	General Electric	6.1
SPERRY	ACQ.	Burroughs	4.9
SAFEWAY STORES	LBO	Kohlberg Kravis Roberts	4.2*
ALLIED STORES	ACQ.	Campeau	3.6*
R. H. MACY	LBO	Macy Acquiring	3.5
MIDCON	ACQ.	Occidental Petroleum	3.0
VIACOM INTERNATIONAL	LBO	Viacom Mgmt., First Boston, DLJ, and Drexel Burnham	3.0*
TEXAS OIL & GAS	ACQ.	USX	3.0
CELANESE	ACQ.	American Hoechst	2.8*
HOLIDAY	RECAP.		2.8*
CONTEL	ACQ.	Communications Satellite	2.5*
ASSOCIATED DRY GOODS	ACQ.	May Department Stores	2.5*
UNION CARBIDE	RECAP.		2.5*
OWENS-CORNING	RECAP.		2.3
FMC	RECAP.		2.2
METROMEDIA TV STATIONS	ACQ.	News America Holdings	2.0

Table 5.1 (Continued)

Company	Type of deal	Buyer	Amount (billions of dollars)
LBO=LEVERAGED BUYOUT		ACQ.=ACQUISITION	
RECAP.=RECAPITALIZATION			
IPO=INITIAL PUBLIC OFFERING		JV=JOINT VENTURE	
COLT INDUSTRIES	RECAP.		1.9
GENSTAR	ACQ.	Imasco	1.8
GROUP W CABLE	ACQ.	GWCI	1.7
LEAR SIEGLER	ACQ.	Wickes	1.7*
COCA-COLA BOTTLING	IPO		1.6*
NATIONAL GYPSUM	LBO	Aancor Holdings	1.6
JACK ECKERD	LBO	Eckerd Holdings	1.6
MGM/UA ENTERTAINMENT	ACQ.	Turner Broadcasting	1.5
TENNECO'S INSURANCE DIV.	ACQ.	ICH	1.5*
ITT'S TELECOMMUNI-CATIONS DIV.	JV	Compagnie Générale d'Electricité	1.5*
UNION CARBIDE'S BATTERY DIV.	ACQ.	Ralston Purina	1.4
JTL	ACQ.	Coca-Cola	1.4
FRUEHAUF	LBO	LMC Acquisition	1.3
METROMEDIA'S CELLULAR TELEPHONE DIV.	ACQ.	Southwestern Bell	1.2*

Table 5.1 (Continued)

Company	Type of deal	Buyer	Amount (billions of dollars)
LBO=LEVERAGED BUYOUT		ACQ.=ACQUISITION	
	RECAP.=RECAPITALIZATION		
IPO=INITIAL PUBLIC OFFERING		JV=JOINT VENTURE	
CONTAINER CORP. OF AMERICA	LBO	JSC/MS Holdings	1.2
SANDERS ASSOCIATES	ACQ.	Lockheed	1.2
COLLINS & AIKMAN	ACQ.	Wickes	1.2
CROCKER NATIONAL	ACQ.	Wells Fargo	1.1
BIG THREE INDUSTRIES	ACQ.	L'Air Liquide	1.1
EX-CELL-O	ACQ.	Textron	1.0
BEATRICE'S BOTTLING DIV.	ACQ.	Coca-Cola	1.0

*Transaction pending.

SOURCE: Reprinted from November 24, 1986 issue of *Business Week* by special permission, © 1986 by McGraw-Hill, Inc.

THE HOW AND WHY OF MERGER MANIA

The current wave of mergers and acquisitions is not the first such boom in American business history. However, the intensity of current merger activity has captured the attention of business analysts, legislators, and even everyday citizens in a way never before seen. The names of the leading raiders (Icahn, Pickens, Jacobs, Turner, and Goldsmith) and deal-makers (Boesky, Siegel, and Levine) have become household words. Merger mania has even sprouted its own colorful vocabulary of tactics to describe the rules of the game: poison pills are swallowed, golden parachutes fly freely, white knights come to the rescue, or a Pac-man defense may be used.[2]

Although watching merger mania may be the hottest spectator sport of the eighties, there is a real concern that danger lurks behind the headlines. Regulators in Washington are torn between allowing the free market to run its course (wherever that takes us) or intervening to put a limit on further activity. At the root of this decision lies real confusion over the motivations for merger mania and the ultimate implications of such activity for the entire economy.[3]

Anxiety over merger activity partly reflects the poor track record such deals have produced for the companies that participate. The current wave of acquisitions has sparked research interest in studying how successful such deals are in creating wealth for shareholders. Most studies agree that acquisitions are a losing proposition. Corporations typically lose about 1 to 10% of their market value during the year following a merger or acquisition. A study by McKinsey & Co. indicates that most firms could do far better by simply putting their money in the bank and collecting interest. Not surprisingly, many corporate marriages end in divorce. Approximately one-third of all acquisitions are eventually un-done.[4]

If acquisitions are so bad, why do them? The poor track record does not seem to deter corporations from playing the acquisitions game. To understand the motivation for mergers and acquisitions, one must look beyond the profit motive and question the goals and objectives of the managers who make merger and acquisition decisions.

WHO'S IN CHARGE HERE?

In theory, managers are the agents of stockholders and are obliged to do their bidding. This means that managers should strive to implement strategies to maximize the profits of the firm. Otherwise, the owners (shareholders) will simply fire the management team and replace them with others who are more cooperative. Unfortunately, the real world is more complex than the theory might indicate. In practice, profits are not the only objective of the firm. The pursuit of other goals is a driving force behind unprofitable mergers and acquisitions.

It is unrealistic to think of a firm as a unified entity in single-minded pursuit of one goal. The "company" itself is an abstract entity with no particular goals or objectives. A more correct view of firms is that they are composed of coalitions of people. The people in companies do have objectives. However, these objectives are likely to be as diverse as the individuals who have them.

The weighting of any individual's goals on the ultimate behavior of the firm is proportional to the power that person holds in the organization. Most shareholders would agree that maximizing profits is a highly desirable goal. However, this goal will not be pursued to the exclusion of the preferences of other people with vested interests in the organization: managers, workers, bankers, and so on. In particular, managers may find that a conflict of interest exists between doing what's best for the shareholders (maximizing profits) and doing what's best for themselves (huge bonuses and lavish perquisites). This conflict is the essence of the debate over the appropriateness of takeover defenses (such as poison pills) and whether or not corporate raiders should be allowed to continue the takeover binge they have initiated during the last few years.[5]

This debate made the front pages during the intense takeover battle between Martin Marietta and Bendix. The bidding war took on almost comical proportions and led to speculation that emotions had taken over to the exclusion of any rational behavior. Bendix first made a tender offer for Martin Marietta in 1982. Marietta responded with the "Pac-Man defense" of making a counteroffer to acquire Bendix. In the end, Bendix owned 67% of Martin Marietta while Martin Marietta owned 60% of Bendix. United Technologies then threw its hat into the ring and tried to rescue Martin Marietta by acquiring Bendix. The eventual winner was Allied, who bought all of Bendix and 39% of Martin Marietta. Lee

Iacocca, chairman of Chrysler, commented on the spectacle: "It's not a merger. It's a three ring circus. If they're really concerned about America, they'd stop it right now. It's no good for the economy. It wrecks it. If I were in the banking system I'd say no more [money] for conglomerates for one year." A former director at Bendix elaborated: "I think . . . it's the kind of thing corporate America ought not to do, because the poor shareholder is the one whose interest is being ignored in favor of the egos of directors and executives. And who the hell is running the show—the business of making brakes and aerospace equipment—while all of this is going on?" Interestingly, the stock prices for both Bendix and Martin Marietta gained from the battle; only Allied's stockholders ended up as losers.

This conflict of interest is very relevant to understanding merger mania. In modern large corporations, no single shareholder is likely to own as much as 5% of the firm. Instead, ownership is thinly spread among literally millions of investors, none of whom can exert any real influence on decision-making. In many cases, the largest single owner is an institution, such as an insurance company or pension fund, which views the stock in purely financial terms. There is no desire or willingness to engage in active decision-making. Major decisions are left to management to make. This gives them the possibility of seeking their own goals to the contrary of shareholder interests.

One such goal is empire building. Managers may seek to create a larger corporation in order to enhance their personal power, to gain prestige, to rationalize a larger salary, or simply because it's fun. Some observers have even compared the passions and emotions behind merger mania to the needs of a drug addict or compulsive gambler. The thrill of the hunt and the joy of consummating a takeover may supersede any rational motives for embarking on an acquisition binge.

PORTRAIT OF A RAIDER: CARL ICAHN

Today's corporate raiders are the 1980s answer to the robber barons of a century ago. One of the most successful of the modern raiders is Carl Icahn. Nearly a decade ago, Icahn decided to buy stock in companies where a proxy fight—or the threat of one—might drive share prices up. That strategy has so far produced profits of over $400 million. As shown in Table 5.2, the list of companies attacked by the Icahn machine reads like a list of who's who in American business.

Carl Icahn has clearly found a winning formula for raiding chosen companies. His impact on those firms is not so clear. Icahn has been labeled both saint and rapist. At one extreme is the argument that Icahn and his fellow raiders play a crucial role in a free market economy. If a firm becomes inefficient and poorly managed, it is ripe for an outsider (like Icahn) to acquire the company, liquidate unproductive assets, perhaps fire unneeded people, shut down antiquated factories, and make the firm competitive again. On the other hand,

Table 5.2 A Deal-Maker's Winning Streak.

Company	Year	Icahn's position	Profits ($ mil)
Baird & Warner	1978	Wins proxy fight for this REIT; renamed Bayswater Realty, it becomes his deal-making vehicle	NM*
Tappan	1979	Wages proxy fight that forces 1979 sale of Ohio stovemaker to Sweden's Electrolux	$3
Saxon	1981	Sells 9.5% stake to copier company at premium, shortly before a scandal depresses stock price	2
Simplicity Pattern	1981	Arranges first bank financing for a takover bid; another raider eventually gains control	7
Anchor Hocking	1982	Buys a 6% stake and sells it back to company one month later, doubling his money	3
American Can	1982	Earns greenmail when company buys 1 million shares from him and pays 30% above market	7

*NM = Not meaningful (private company, gain cannot be calculated).

Table 5.2 (Continued)

Company	Year	Icahn's position	Profits ($ mil)
Marshall Field	1982	Joins group that accumulates 30% stake, which forces retailer to sell to Britain's BAT Industries	18
Gulf & Western	1983	Buys 3 million shares at $22; sells in the open market two months later at $29	20
Dan River	1983	Builds stock position and makes takeover threats, which lead to leveraged buyout	9
ACF	1983	Spends $405 million to acquire rail-car builder, topping the bid of leveraged buyout firm	NM
Chesebrough–Pond's	1984	Does a deal: Company buys his 5% stake at no premium—and an ACF division for $95 million	6
Uniroyal	1984	Sells 10% stake to company, which then goes private through a leveraged buyout	13

Table 5.2 (Continued)

Company	Year	Icahn's position	Profits ($ mil)
Goodrich	1984	Receives a greenmail payment that is 25% above market for his just-under-5% stake	10
Phillips Petroleum	1985	Offers $8 billion to acquire company, but later sells stake when it borrows to restructure	35
TWA	1985	Invests $400 million and gains control; as chairman, he cuts costs and improves earnings	100*
Union Carbide	1986	Builds stock position in first quarter and sells to company when it restructures	40
Viacom	1986	Trades his 17% stake to the company for cash, securities, and free advertising for TWA	40
USX	1986	Buys an 11% stake and gets junk bond financing for $8 billion takeover offer	120*

*Paper profit, gain not yet realized.

SOURCE: Reprinted from October 27, 1986 issue of *Business Week* by special permission, © 1986 by McGraw-Hill, Inc.

such tactics have a human cost. A recent target of Icahn is USX Corporation (formerly U.S. Steel). Richard Caliguiri, mayor of Pittsburgh, where USX is based, labeled Icahn "a quick buck artist . . . [who] takes millions of dollars out of corporations and destroys them."

What does a raider do? Icahn sees his role as both manager and catalyst for change. He looks for companies that are poorly managed and that are underutilizing their assets. Icahn sees himself as an outsider who is unafraid to make the difficult changes sometimes needed to restore the competitiveness of weak firms. His claim is that entrenched managers are more concerned about their personal empires and bonus checks than confronting the realities of the competitive marketplace. Layoffs and plant closings may be painful medicine to swallow, but they are a necessary evil to restore efficient production.

The "victims" of his raids don't see it that way. They view his acquisitions as motivated by short-term financial gains. The chairman of Goodyear, Robert Mercer, calls such raids "economic terrorism." Workers become pawns in a gambit for capital gains. They expect Icahn to take the money and run, not to stick around for the long haul. Do the raiders hurt or help the companies they acquire?

The truth is somewhere in between. Icahn can point to some conspicuous successes. Icahn acquired TWA in 1986 when the firm was in serious trouble. The airline was losing about $1 million per day and heading for bankruptcy. Icahn's critics concluded that he had finally erred. Icahn's $400 million investment looked like a lost cause. However, Icahn surprised everyone with his dramatic turnaround of TWA. During the last half of 1986, TWA earned approximately $75 million, while competing airlines continued to flounder.

Icahn's salvation of TWA resulted from drastic cost-cutting and improved operating efficiency. His cuts hit every level of the organization, from corporate officers to flight attendants. He took a hard line with labor: When senior flight attendants went on strike, he hired young replacements at a fraction of the salary. Pilots and machinists took pay cuts of up to 26%. The result was a new company with far greater ability to compete in a highly competitive industry.

Nonetheless, even Carl Icahn would admit that making a fast buck is part of the game. In several cases, firms have paid Icahn millions of dollars to refrain from making a hostile takeover. American Can paid Icahn $7 million in 1982. For Goodrich, the price was $10 million in 1984. Icahn's booty is not unique. Other raiders have received even higher payoffs (some would say bribes) to refrain from making an acquisition. In November 1986, Gillette chairman Colman Mockler paid $558 million to buy out the holdings of Ronald Perelman, chief executive officer of Revlon. Goodyear bought out raider Sir James Goldsmith for approximately $620 million to avoid a takeover. Goldsmith netted $90 million on the deal.

Icahn's latest venture is USX. His acquisition of 11% of America's largest steel company has raised concerns that he may have finally bitten off more than he can chew. Only time will tell if Icahn's luck will continue to hold.

Merger mania is not confined to the boardroom. Individual investors have learned that the profits from correctly anticipating the takeover of a firm can be enormous. (See box.) One study found that approximately one-third of all investors in the stock market cited acquisition activity as a criterion for selecting investments. Although the potential rewards are high, one might be better off at the gaming tables at Las Vegas. It is extremely difficult to anticipate a takeover before it is announced. Investments based on rumors found in the financial pages are similar to a crapshoot. The only sure-fire technique for success is to act on insider information. However, the risks are even higher with this strategy. Dennis Levine, an investment banker with a salary of roughly $1 million per year, made an estimated $12 million in profits from insider trading but was later convicted on four felony charges. Ivan Boesky, one of the most active arbitrageurs on Wall Street, found himself in similar straits. Boesky was slapped with $100 million in fines and was forced to retire permanently from the securities business.

HOW TO FIND, SPECULATE ON HOT TAKEOVER RUMORS

They're called "story stocks."
On Wall Street lately, the big story has been story stocks—ABC Corp. stock jumps on takeover speculation; DEF Co. soars because a management buyout is

anticipated; a rumored restructuring drives up GHI Inc.

"Any time you get a market in a confused state like this, the story stocks are going to be hot," said Carol Morrow, market strategist at Piper, Jaffray & Hopwood Inc.

Given that the vast majority of stocks are languishing, small investors may be tempted to look for a seat on one of the bandwagons.

It certainly looks easy enough:

■ On Oct. 7, Goodyear Tire & Rubber Co. jumped 3 to $36⅞. The rumor: GAF Corp. Chairman Samuel Heyman might make a bid. That hasn't come to pass, but now a British investor is said to be readying a bid. Friday's close: $48⅝. If you'd bought after the first report, you'd have a 32% paper profit.

■ On Oct. 6, Transworld Corp. rose 1⅞ to $27¾. It was a takeover candidate, analysts said—and they were right. Now the company is considering ways to restructure to fight off raider Ronald Perelman. Friday's close: $41½—a 50% gain since the early rumors.

But seldom is it that simple, experts warn. For every Goodyear or Transworld there are dozens such as Jim Walter Corp. (which rose to $54⅝ in September on rumors Wickes Cos. was about to bid, but has fallen to $45⅛) and Texas American Bancshares (which hit $25½ as takeover fever swept Texas banks in September; now it's $18¾).

"It's a pretty unforgiving market when there are disappointments or the action switches elsewhere," said William Tichy, analyst at Dean Witter Reynolds Inc.

Small investors operate at a disadvantage because they're often the last to get information—good or bad. And big investors pay lower trading commissions, so it's easier for them to move money around.

But for the nimble investor, the takeover market may hold opportunities, said Walter Jurek, president of Quality Services Inc. Earlier this year, the company started the Santa Barbara Fund to invest in takeover candidates. The fledgling mutual fund turned in the top performance among non-gold stock funds in the third quarter. Its gain: 18.8%.

To play takeover rumors, experts advise:

■ Be patient if you buy. Between Oct. 1 and 2, Hazeltine Corp. jumped 3 to $22⅝ on buyout rumors. For three weeks nothing happened. The price fell to $20⅛ on Oct. 23. Four days later, Hazeltine agreed to a $30-a-share buyout by Emerson Electric Co.

■ Set a stop-loss point. "The first 10% you lose is the safest 10% to lose," Jurek said. The risk: In Hazeltine's case, you would have missed the eventual deal.

■ Don't be too greedy. If a stock has risen 30% from its previous range, "It's pretty well maxed out for the short-term," Jurek said.

■ When rumors swirl around a company, immediately think about others in the industry. They may attract attention too. Example: A rumored bid for E.F. Hutton Group has sent speculators after Merrill Lynch and PaineWebber Group lately.

Indeed, an unsuccessful raider often looks for another, similar target. After Wickes lost its bid for National Gypsum Co. in April, it made a run for

> Owens-Corning Fiberglas Corp. When that offer was spurned, speculators rushed into two other building-supply companies: Jim Walter and USG Corp. So far, nothing has come of it all. USG, which peaked at $46½, closed Friday at $40⅜.
>
> ■ Follow a target. If a company's stock retreats significantly after fighting off a takeover, it may present a buying opportunity, Jurek said. Reason: "Management may get the message and work to get the stock price up." If not, another raider may appear.

SOURCE: Copyright 1986, USA TODAY. Reprinted with permission.

Raiders and arbitrageurs are not the only ones to make a fortune from merger mania. Perhaps the most enviable position of all is with the brokers—the investment bankers who take no risks, yet pocket tremendous commissions. Wall Street yuppies are earning mind-boggling brokerage fees from bringing together merger partners. The three leading investment banks (Goldman Sachs, First Boston, and Morgan Stanley) pulled in over $200 million in broker's fees in 1985, not including commissions for helping to raise the money to finance deals.[6]

The emergence of the billion-dollar mergers of the eighties has been accompanied by equally glamorous investment banker fees. The work is hard, but the rewards are enormous. For example, when Baxter Travenol acquired American Hospital Supply in 1985, investment bankers worked nearly round the clock for a month to iron out the details. The result: a $15.5 million fee to split between Goldman Sachs and First Boston. These fees trickle down into enormous salaries for the staff. Many investment bankers in their early thirties have become millionaires within a few years of finishing graduate school.

BEYOND MERGER MANIA

Despite the leadership and power exerted by top management in making acquisitions, they are still denied any true ownership in the resulting firm. However, during the last few years a managerial innovation has emerged to address this problem: the leveraged buyout.[7]

A leveraged buyout (LBO) is a means for managers to buy a company from its stockholders and to run it as a privately owned enterprise. A group of managers can buy their firm by offering to purchase the outstanding shares at a premium over the going market price. Interestingly, this purchase can be made with little or no financing from the managers involved. They simply borrow the required funds using the firm's assets and cash flow as collateral. Joseph Perella, an investment banker at First Boston, remarked as he pulled out his wallet and threw a fistfull of cash into the air: "In the old days you used to need some of this. Not any more!" When managers purchase a firm, the buyout is *leveraged* because the company is usually placed heavily in debt in order to buy back the stock. In many cases, the funds are raised through highly speculative "junk bonds" (IOUs with low-quality ratings) that load the firm up with debt and can jeopardize the future solvency of the company.

Such risks have not curtailed LBO activity. Leveraged buyouts have existed for over a decade, but only recently have they become a common practice. One study in the mid-1970s estimated that the average market value of the 45 companies that proposed a buyout was only $3 million. The deals today commonly go into the billions. The volume of LBOs rose from $1 billion in 1980 to over $11 billion by 1984 and is still going up. The driving force behind this trend is the huge windfall that executives can reap from a successful LBO.

An example of the potential rewards to managers from a buyout is the case of Gibson Greeting Cards. William Simon, former Treasury Secretary in the Nixon and Ford administrations, led a group of investors who purchased Gibson from RCA in 1982. Simon's group put up $1 million of their own money and borrowed an additional $79 million against Gibson's assets. They turned Gibson into a private firm and reorganized its operations. After 18 months, they sold $290 million of Gibson stock to the general public. Simon's share of ownership was over $65 million. The Gibson deal was not unique. Simon runs a firm specializing in leveraged buyouts. Of the roughly 20 deals put together by his firm, six have gone the full circle of leveraged buyout to sell-off. Simon's firm invested $14 million in the initial LBO of these six companies. The proceeds from the eventual public offerings were over $445 million. Table

5.3 shows the enormous potential profits for executives who pull off a successful leveraged buyout.

Not every LBO creates a windfall. Thatcher Glass Corporation was bought from Dart & Kraft in 1981 for $140 million. Three years later it filed for bankruptcy and sold off most of its assets for $40 million. Numerous creditors were left holding the bag, including five of the original LBO lenders who were owed over $77 million.

Acquisition activity has also reached American soil from abroad. At the end of 1985, foreign owners held 10% or more of companies that accounted for 8.5% of all American sales. In some industries, the figures are particularly high: Foreign owners control 33% of American sales in chemicals and over 12% in metals. These are not imports; they are American firms now under foreign ownership and control. As shown in Figure 5.1, foreign purchases of American companies have risen from $2 billion in 1983 to roughly $18 billion in 1986. Some of the deals are enormous: In 1986, the West German chemical firm Hoechst agreed to buy Celanese for $2.8 billion in cash. The French industrial gas producer L'Air Liquide bought Big Three Industries for over $1.1 billion. White Consolidated and Fairchild Semiconductor also passed into the hands of foreign owners.

WHERE DOES THIS TAKE US?

Much ink has been spilled on speculations about where this boom in merger and acquisition activity is likely to take us. Will mergers and acquisitions leave American

Table 5.3 Miraculous Changes in Market Value.

Company	LBO price Date	Value when taken public or sold	Percentage increase
Beatrice	$6.2 billion 4/86	$10 billion (est.) Assets sold: Avis for $1.6 billion; Coke bottling unit for $1 billion; 80% of International Playtex for $1.25 billion; other businesses for $2.15 billion	61%
Blue Bell	$470 million 11/84	$792 million Sold to VF Corp. for $378 million in cash and stock plus assumption of $414 million in long-term debt	69%
Dr Pepper	$650 million 2/84	$866 million Assets sold: Canada Dry for $175 million; bottling plants and other businesses sold for $215 million; Dr Pepper sold for $416 million	33%
Leslie Fay	$58 million 4/82	$360 million Taken public again 8/86	521%
Lily Tulip	$180 million 3/81	$326 million Sold to Owens-Illinois 4/86	81%
Metromedia	$1.1 billion 6/84	$6.5 billion (est.) Assets sold: seven TV stations for $2 billion; cellular radio business for $1.1 billion; other businesses worth $2.4 billion	490%

Table 5.3 (Continued)

Company	LBO price Date	Value when taken public or sold	Percentage increase
Fred Meyer	$420 million 12/81	$900 million (est.) Retailing operation worth $380 million when taken public 4/86; real estate estimated at over $500 million	114%
SFN	$450 million 2/85	$1.1 billion (est.) Assets sold: Scott Foresman for $520 million; South-Western Publishing for $270 million; TV and radio stations for $154 million	144%
Uniroyal	$900 million 9/85	$1.4 billion (est.) Assets sales pending: chemicals business for $750 million; other businesses for $350 million; estimated net worth of the rest of the company is $422 million	55%

Since 1981, 260 public companies have gone private. Of those, some 30 or so have been taken public again or broken up and the assets sold off. The average increase in value for the 30 between being bought and being sold again is about 150%. Managers made out like gangbusters.

SOURCE: *Fortune*, 19 January. © 1987 Time Inc. All rights reserved.

companies more efficient and better able to compete? Or will they strip them of their most valuable assets?

The threat of hostile acquisition has forced many managers to scramble for protection. In some cases, this can take productive forms: Fat is trimmed, losing products are abandoned, and the reality of tough foreign competition is fully confronted. But there are dangers as well. In many industries, mergers are creating greater concentration and the risks of monopoly power. For example, the top six firms in the airline industry now control roughly 84% of the market. In other markets, several of the largest competitors merged: Nestlé purchased Carnation, Burroughs purchased Sperry, General Electric bought RCA, and Wells Fargo bought Crocker National Bank. The Reagan administration has taken a more liberal view of intraindustry mergers than previous administrations. So far, there is little evidence to suggest that the recent wave of mergers will create monopoly power in affected markets, but only time will tell for sure.

There is also concern that the latest wave of mergers has left many companies financially unstable. When the US economy enters the next recession, many firms may find themselves in financial distress as a result of heavy debt loads used to finance acquisitions in the early eighties. Low interest rates and ample cash at lending institutions made it easy to secure potentially imprudent lines of credit to make highly leveraged acquisitions. Those same loans may come back to haunt many firms if the American economy returns to the environment of the seventies.[8]

While merger mania has the potential to make American business leaner and meaner, it may also have the opposite effect. American businesspeople have been accused of myopia for years. Unlike their Japanese counterparts, American executives seem preoccupied with short-run earnings performance. If a new product or strategy can't show a quick result, it will be abandoned. This obsession with the near term sacrifices long-run competitive positioning and can ultimately lead to the downfall of the firm.

Merger mania may reinforce this problem. When firms become embroiled in a takeover battle, such as the Bendix/Martin Marietta fiasco, they ignore the day-to-day business of running the company. Managers get caught up in a whirlwind of moves and countermoves until a final deal is struck. Unfortunately, when one deal is finished, they move on to another one.

EXECUTIVE SUMMARY

- Merger and acquisition activity is at an all-time high.
- The motives for takeovers are not always pure. Mergers and acquisitions based on greed and empire building can be devastating to corporations and the people who work at them.

- Corporate raiders have emerged as major power brokers in the US economy. The mere threat of a hostile takeover can send shockwaves through a potential target.

- Foreign acquisitions of American firms are also booming. A significant fraction of American workers now have foreign bosses.

ENDNOTES

1. See, for example, *Business Week*, 26 November 1986 and 3 June 1985.
2. See *Fortune*, 11 November 1985, for a description of these tactics.
3. An excellent discussion of this debate appears in Jensen's article in the *Harvard Business Review*, November–December 1984.
4. Some additional statistics appear in *Business Week*, 3 June 1985.
5. A fuller description of the issues relating to managerial control of firms can be found in Scherer, *Industrial Market Structure and Economic Performance*. New York: Rand McNally, 1980.
6. For more information, see "Merger Fees That Bend the Mind," in *Fortune*, 20 January 1986.
7. Some of the motivations can be found in *Business Week*, 27 June 1983.
8. For some of the changes in LBO strategies for the future, see L. Lowenstein, "No More Cozy Management Buy-outs," *Harvard Business Review*, January–February 1986.

6

THE OTHER SIDE OF MERGER MANIA: BREAKING UP IS HARD TO DO

The merger boom of the eighties has been accompanied by an equally spectacular boom in divestitures and corporate liquidations. Companies are restructuring their business portfolios by eliminating unproductive assets and concentrating their resources on areas of top priority. In some cases, one company's divestiture will become another firm's acquisition. Sometimes the strategy is more drastic; an operation can be totally shut down: Plants are closed, equipment is sold, and jobs are permanently eliminated. In many cases, divestitures are previous acquisitions that didn't work out. A study by the consulting firm McKinsey and Company indicated that approximately one-third of all acquisitions eventually are undone.

TRENDS

The last great boom in acquisitions occurred during the 1960s. This was the era of conglomerate building. Many of the motives discussed in the previous chapter were the driving forces behind the conglomerate empire building of the 1960s. The prevailing attitude was "bigger is better," and many acquisitions were consummated with little consideration of how well the partners would fit together as a combined entity. These shotgun weddings often end in divorce. It is far easier to close a deal on an acquisition than to make one work successfully. To some extent, the latest wave of divestitures is the fallout from the conglomerate boom of the late 1960s.[1]

Conglomerate strategies of the 1960s were often built on a house of cards. Great fortunes were built through a pyramid scheme of stock price manipulation. Acquisitions gave the appearance of growth, and the appearance of growth gave a firm access to capital to finance more acquisitions. The conglomerate boom was fueled by a strong stock market, which made it easy to issue new equity and raise funds. During the sixties, the mentality of investors was to reward growth above all other factors. This encouraged firms to make rapid acquisitions in order to boost their apparent performance. As a result, a peculiar cycle of incentives and rewards was created. A firm with a high growth rate (such as a conglomerate) was rewarded with a high price-to-earnings (P/E) ratio. A high P/E ratio makes it cheaper to secure funds for more acquisitions. If a high P/E firm (such as the high-growth conglomerates of the sixties) acquires a low P/E firm, the earnings per share of the conglomerate will automatically go up.

ILLUSIONS OF GROWTH

This creates the illusion that the conglomerate is both high growth (due to the greater combined revenues of the two firms) and profitable (due to higher earnings per share). This apparent high performance is simply the result of the way accountants handle the books for an acquisition. Nonetheless, the charade continued for many years and led to some of the largest conglomerate empires in the world. A closer look at the true performance of these firms indicates that the increased growth and profits were usually artificial. After adjusting for the acquisition, the true performance of the underlying businesses was generally quite poor. Consequently, the stock market became far more skeptical of conglomerate strategies and began to price conglomerates at a discount relative to other firms. In fact, during the last 15 years, conglomerates have usually exhibited lower return on equity and lower P/E ratios than other types of firms.

A great deal of research has been directed at trying to understand why conglomerate strategies have proven so unsuccessful. In their book *In Search of Excellence*, Peters and Waterman studied the strategies and performance of successful American companies and tried to uncover patterns to account for their success. One of their key findings was that the most successful firms tend to "stick to the knitting." In other words, firms that identify a core set of skills and capabilities and focus their strategies around a central theme tend to outperform the companies that are widely diversified and spread themselves too thin. A seminal study by Richard Rumelt came to a similar conclusion. He found that "related diversification" strategies were consistently more profitable than conglomerate strategies. A related diversification strategy means that a company will only invest in lines of business that are closely related to other parts of its operations.[2]

Many firms have come to the same conclusion through the school of hard knocks. The statistics are impressive. According to merger and acquisition specialists W.T. Grimm and Company, divestitures rose 40% in the early 1980s. The increase in average size was even more impressive. The dollar value of divestitures rose to over $29 billion, more than double the level of the late 1970s. As shown in Figure 5.1 in the last chapter and Table 6.1 below, divestiture strategies are being adopted by some of the largest corporations in America.[3]

ITT was considered by many to be the ultimate conglomerate. Under the leadership of Harold Geneen, ITT made hundreds of acquisitions during the sixties and seventies. In 1968, during the height of the conglomerate boom, ITT's stock sold at a P/E multiple of more than 20. By 1980, ITT's stock was selling at less than five times earnings, and confidence in the conglomerate strategy had sunk to an all-time low. Today, ITT is busily restructuring its business portfolio to give their operations a theme. They have sold over 100 subsidiaries and are concentrating their efforts on a few carefully selected sectors.

Table 6.1 Look Who's Been Crowding the Corporate Divorce Court.

Seller	Unit sold	Buyer	Year	Price
GENERAL ELECTRIC	Utah International	Broken Hill Proprietary	1983	$2.4 billion
R. J. REYNOLDS INDUSTRIES	Aminoil	Phillips Petroleum	1984	$1.7 billion
RCA	CIT Financial	Manufacturers Hanover	1983	$1.5 billion
CITY INVESTING	Uarco, Rheem Mfg., World Color Press	Management buyout led by Kohlberg Kravis Roberts	1984	$1.3 billion
TEXACO	Employers Reinsurance	General Electric	1984	$1.1 billion
GULF & WESTERN*	Simmons, Kayser-Roth, other consumer and industrial units	Wickes	1985	$1 billion
UNITED TECHNOLOGIES*	Inmont	BASF	1985	$1 billion
ALLEGHENY	Investors Diversified Services	American Express	1983	$829 million

Table 6.1 (Continued)

Seller	Unit sold	Buyer	Year	Price
KIEWIT-MURDOCH INVESTMENT	Florida Gas Transmission	Houston Natural Gas	1984	$800 million
BEATRICE	Chemical operations	Imperial Chemical Industries	1984	$750 million
CHEVRON	Some Gulf stations, refinery	Standard Oil of Ohio	1984	$690 million
DUN & BRADSTREET	Corinthian Broadcasting	A. H. Belo	1983	$606 million
DU PONT	Some chemical assets	Management buyout led by E. F. Hutton	1983	$600 million
GENERAL ELECTRIC	Family Financial Services	Philadelphia Saving Fund Society	1984	$600 million
OCCIDENTAL PETROLEUM	Refinery, gas stations, other facilities	Southland	1983	$582 million
RCA*	Hertz	UAL	1985	$578 million

*Pending

Table 6.1 (Continued)

Seller	Unit sold	Buyer	Year	Price
CITY INVESTING	Motel 6	Management buyout led by Kohlberg Kravis Roberts	1984	$565 million
HUSKY OIL OF CANADA	Husky Oil (U.S. unit)	U.S. Steel	1984	$505 million
ITT	Continental Baking	Ralston Purina	1984	$475 million
DOW CHEMICAL	50% of Dowell oilfield services business	Schlumberger	1984	$440 million
INTERNATIONAL HARVESTER	Farm equipment	Tenneco	1984	$430 million
WALTER E. HELLER INTERNATIONAL	Walter E. Heller & Co., Heller Overseas	Fuji Bank	1983	$425 million
HOUSTON NATURAL GAS	Liquid Carbonic	CBI Industries	1984	$407 million
TEXAS EASTERN	Transwestern Pipeline	Houston Natural Gas	1984	$390 million
CONTINENTAL GROUP	Most container board and kraft paper operations	Stone Container	1983	$390 million

SOURCE: Reprinted from July 1, 1985 issue of *Business Week* by special permission, © 1985 by McGraw-Hill.

Fuqua Industries is another case in point. Fuqua Industries was founded by J. B. Fuqua, who built an empire of trucking, radio and TV stations, movie theaters, recreational products, petroleum distribution, lawnmowers, and other assorted businesses. More recently, Fuqua has been eliminating many of these operations and concentrating on a handful of products. According to the chairman, "[in the past] . . . when we made an acquisition, the stock went up. So we went out and made acquisitions." Today, the rewards are generally in the other direction. The result: Fuqua's restructuring strategy has led to a doubling of its stock price since 1980.[4]

STRATEGIC COMPLEXITY PREVAILS

The booms in mergers and divestitures are intertwined. One firm's divestiture is another firm's acquisition. As firms recreate their identities, they often become more attractive as acquisition targets. For example, RCA began focusing on its electronics businesses in the early 1980s and divested its holdings in CIT Financial and Hertz rental cars. This made RCA into a pure electronics and broadcasting company, very similar to the initial strategy of the original Radio Corporation of America prior to its diversification fling of the sixties and seventies. Meanwhile, General Electric was embarking on a similar strategy. Under the leadership of Jack Welch, GE has made over 70 acquisitions and 190 divestitures to redeploy its assets more cleanly into a few focused areas.

As part of this strategy, GE acquired RCA in one of the largest acquisitions of all time. It is likely that a more diversified RCA would not have attracted GE's attention.

Welch's restructuring of GE is already starting to bear fruit. He has raised over $6 billion from divestitures and spent more than $10 billion on new acquisitions. In some ways, GE is a microcosm of what is happening in the US economy. The company got its start in 1878 to exploit the inventions of Thomas Edison. Over the following decades, GE grew to massive size, becoming a dominant competitor in literally hundreds of markets. GE also became widely respected as a model of "professional management," always on the cutting edge of the newest business school techniques.

However, tradition and raw size were not enough to enable the company to survive against vigorous competition from abroad. During the last ten years, GE has been challenged in nearly every one of its markets and in many cases has come up on the losing end. The company came to the conclusion that it was spread too thin and needed more focus in order to become successful again. GE has chosen to concentrate on selected high-technology and service businesses, which it believes it can dominate over the long term. When GE evaluated which businesses it wanted to sell or retain, it applied a simple criterion: In order to remain a part of the firm, a business had to be number one or number two in its market. The strategy seems to be working. GE has increased its earnings by 54% from 1980 through 1985 and seems well positioned for growth in the future. Consequently, the stock price has gone from $30 to $80 per share.

However, not everyone is pleased with the changes at GE. A central part of Welch's overhaul was to cut costs, particularly in labor. This led to the elimination of over *100,000* jobs, more than a quarter of the work force. In the words of one GE executive: "Morale stinks. People are looking for jobs or waiting for a nice severance package . . . . I don't see the greatness that everybody says is here. I could understand if out of this devastation came something we could all look to as the wave of the future. But I see a void." Unfortunately for GE and other firms who engage in massive reorganization, the departure of disgruntled employees is not the cure for poor morale. Those who stay have long memories. It may take many years for the trauma of restructuring to heal.[5]

An interesting sideline to the boom in divestitures is the type of operations that are being sold. Divestitures have been around for many years. However, in the past, divestitures were usually seen as a last resort tactic for getting rid of undesirable parts of a company's business portfolio. The "dogs" were divested in order to concentrate on more profitable lines of business. This is still true today, but many divestitures are very profitable business units. Divestitures are made in order to focus on selected parts of a firm's business, even if other (lower priority) lines of business are quite profitable. The sale of these profitable but unwanted businesses are seen as a means of raising cash and allowing investment in the rest of the firm.

Gulf + Western is an example of a conglomerate that has come full circle. After many years of active acquisitions, Gulf + Western is now selling off major parts of its business in order to concentrate on entertainment, financial services, and information businesses. Many of Gulf + Western's biggest divestitures are businesses it had acquired within the previous ten years. Some of the biggest divestitures are shown in Figure 6.1.

While divestitures involve primarily a change in ownership, liquidations are more extreme. A liquidation occurs when a firm believes that part of the company is worth more at auction in pieces than as an entire operation. When the business unit is liquidated, it is usually dismantled into saleable items such as land, equipment, warehouses, and machines and then sold off on the open market. During the last few years, many firms have been selling in the stock market at less than their book value, thus giving rise to the possibility that the firms were worth more in pieces than as a whole. This is the exact opposite of *synergy*, where it is thought that a combination of assets is worth more than simply the sum of the individual pieces. Several of the leading raiders have gained a reputation for spotting troubled firms that are being dragged down by unprofitable operations. Such firms can be acquired cheaply. The losing operations are liquidated (sometimes at a significant profit), and the remaining business can be operated as a healthy enterprise. Naturally, this tactic wreaks havoc on the people and the organization involved. Most jobs are usually eliminated, and only the most promising core of

Figure 6.1 Restructuring at Gulf + Western.

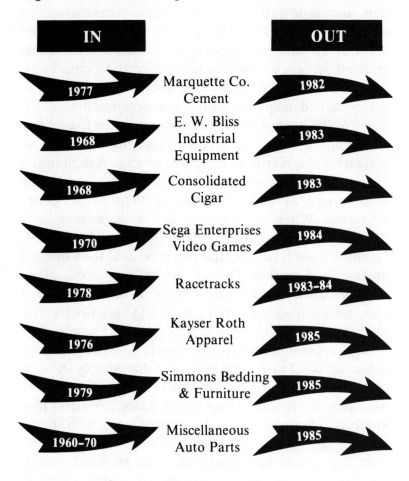

IN		OUT
1977	Marquette Co. Cement	1982
1968	E. W. Bliss Industrial Equipment	1983
1968	Consolidated Cigar	1983
1970	Sega Enterprises Video Games	1984
1978	Racetracks	1983–84
1976	Kayser Roth Apparel	1985
1979	Simmons Bedding & Furniture	1985
1960–70	Miscellaneous Auto Parts	1985

the company is preserved. As a result, raiders using such a strategy have acquired a notorious reputation. Irv "the Liquidator" Jacobs is one of the breed of raiders known for identifying struggling firms with hidden value.

CREATIVE BANKRUPTCY

Another recent tactic is the creative use of bankruptcy laws, often in conjunction with an acquisition. Bankruptcy has traditionally been seen as a last resort for firms that cannot survive on their own. The Chapter 11 provisions are designed to enable a company to continue operating under protection from its creditors in order to allow the firm to regain financial health and (presumably) someday repay its debts.

The bankruptcy laws are now being used by clever managers as simply another management tool. During the last few years, a number of relatively healthy firms have filed for protection under Chapter 11. They have used this law as a means of reducing exposure to large product liability suits or to enhance their bargaining position relative to unions. Manville was the first firm to file for bankruptcy protection at a time when it was relatively solvent. It saw the Chapter 11 provision as a means for protection from the potentially enormous asbestos liability suits facing the firm. A. H. Robins used a similar tactic to protect itself from liability claims arising from sales of their Dalkon shield. In both cases, there were protests that these firms were manipulating the bankruptcy laws in a manner not intended by the courts.[6]

Filing for bankruptcy can also be used to break the power of a union. In 1983, Wilson Foods succeeded in slashing wages by filing for Chapter 11. An even more spectacular example is the use of Chapter 11 provisions by Frank Lorenzo at Continental Airlines. Like many airlines, Continental was caught in a squeeze between vigorous price competition and escalating union demands for high wages. In the five years prior to 1983, Continental had lost over $500 million and was losing money at the rate of $1 million per day. Frank Lorenzo, who has been making airline acquisitions at a rapid pace, recognized the opportunity that the bankruptcy laws provided for wage reduction. Lorenzo put Continental into bankruptcy and forced employees to accept a 50% cut in wages to restore competitiveness. Out of the work force of 11,000 at the time of filing for bankruptcy, over 5,000 were fired or quit. The enormous wage concessions and layoffs had a dramatic effect on Continental's performance. After three years in bankruptcy, Continental was 40% larger and had become one of the industry's most profitable and aggressive operators. The furor over

Continental's use of the bankruptcy laws was so intense that new legislation was passed to make it more difficult to utilize the same tactics in the future. Nonetheless, some industry observers indicate that Continental could have easily passed the more stringent tests, had they been in force.

Continental's tactics are part of a massive restructuring of the entire airline industry (see Figure 6.2). Mergers and takeovers are nearly a daily event. One industry observer remarked:

> I have it on good authority that Delta is buying Eastern. Eastern is buying Pan Am. Pan Am is really going after United now that it has all of the United's cash, and American's Bob Crandall, who has been devilishly silent all along, is getting ready to make a tender offer for the whole industry once he reaches agreement with his pilots.
>
> Furthermore, I spoke to Frank Lorenzo this morning, and he assured me his next targets are Peru and Bolivia, which he plans to merge into the first low-cost country.
>
> —Saloman Brothers analyst
> Julius Maldutis, speaking
> before the Wings Club in New York,
> February 19, 1986.

Unlike the general skepticism about the value of mergers and acquisitions to the economy, many experts

Figure 6.2

'Well, I think we've about seen the end to the takeovers and buy-outs'

SOURCE: Reprinted by permission: Tribune Media Services.

believe that the divestiture boom is improving American competitiveness. There is very little evidence to suggest that conglomerates have done a good job of operating their disparate businesses. One study of 15 businesses divested by conglomerates indicated that all but one have performed better under new ownership. It appears that conglomerates add overhead and expenses, but provide very little assistance to their subsidiaries.

Although the spinning off of corporate assets may prove beneficial in the long run, there is likely to be a painful transition toward a leaner and meaner corporate profile. The wounds of reorganization and restructuring are deep and fresh. The flip side of merger mania has a human cost. For many firms, that is a price that is still to be paid.

EXECUTIVE SUMMARY

- The boom in merger and acquisition activity has been accompanied by an equally spectacular boom in divestiture activity.

- Many current divestitures are the by-products of previous acquisitions that failed.

- Divestitures take a human toll. At General Electric, over 100,000 jobs were eliminated.

- In some cases, unnecessary bankruptcy has been used as a strategy for reducing liabilities and union busting.

ENDNOTES

1. Some of the historical cycles in acquisitions are described in Salter, M. and Weinhold, W., *Diversification through Acquisition: Strategies for Creating Economic Value* (New York: Macmillan, 1979).

2. Rumelt's work broke new ground in understanding the relative performance of different corporate strategies. His analysis goes well beyond the simple issues addressed here.
3. See *Business Week*, 1 July 1985.
4. This sentiment by Fuqua and others appears in *Business Week*, 3 June 1985.
5. An excellent case study of restructuring appears in *Business Week*, 30 June 1986.
6. Some new developments in the use of bankruptcy as a management tool appear in *Business Week*, 16 June 1986.

7

IMPACT: THE COMPANY AND ITS PARTS

When attempting to predict the outcome of post-merger trauma, the first reality one confronts is that the task is nearly impossible. There are too many variables and too many possible combinations of human behavior, personality, and corporate circumstances to enable the observer to predict precise answers and outcomes. It is difficult enough for an outsider to undertake rational and objective analysis of such phenomena. The exercise becomes almost hopelessly impossible for a participant. It is hard to be objective when your job and career are at stake!

Despite the difficulties, we can develop scenarios. First, we can predict areas of fallout, the sectors where trauma will occur. Then we can focus on specific events in those areas. In this chapter, we shall identify several sectors in which mergers will produce change and tension. These areas are:

¶ Leadership and followership
¶ Organizational structure and structural change

¶   Morale and attitudes (organizational climate)

¶   Corporate culture and norms

If one looks for subtle changes within these areas, one will begin to uncover possible results. Within each of the categories there are likely scenarios, each having its own set of conditions, actors, and outcomes. Much like the "games people play," as described by Tom Harris and Eric Berne in their writing on the structure of recurring human interactions (called "transactions"), these scenarios are nearly as predictable as scripts in a play. In looking for signs of merger, acquisition, or other forms of corporate chaos, one should pay attention to these sectors.

LEADERSHIP AND FOLLOWERSHIP

Leadership will most likely follow ownership. Those who hold title also hold the pen to draw the organization chart. However, one cannot assume that owners always want to be in formal positions of leadership.[1] Sometimes they prefer to have a representative.

How does such a principle look when it is played out in the drama of a corporate takeover? When companies merge, *structural consolidation* and *integration* take place. The resulting structure may be "leaner," since personnel and managerial responsibility can now be limited to individuals who emerge as the strongest in the new organization. The same is true for an acquisition. But who determines who will survive in the new structure? What principle underlies these decisions? Most commonly, such decisions are made by senior leaders who govern the emerging structure. These are the managers most in favor with owners and their agents. Predicting who will remain and who will be fired is not always easy. The managers of the acquiring company are not always the most qualified executives, and many critical decisions will be made during the first weeks and months after the deal is struck.

What to observe? Where to look? Some signs are visible and others must be ferreted out.

Consultants are one of the most visible indicators. Sometimes there are prominent consulting teams. Other times, the "consulting factor" is one person, typically a senior man whom the "oldtimers" in the company will relate to as a confidant. These seasoned outsiders and consultants are poor sources of information, for they are often trained to fend off any suspicious inquiries. On the other hand, junior consultants can be an excellent source of information. If junior consultants are seen in the organization, they are often working on data collection at very low levels. They may have extensive knowledge about the purpose of their study and be eager to socialize.

Often a direct query will produce a knee-jerk response that an activity must be clandestine. Much has been written about the rumor mill and how powerful the informal organization can become at critical, high-stress times.[2] Employees can learn much from the pool of rumors, but caution is advised. Most rumors must be discounted because their sources are biased and inaccurate. They often derive more from wish than from truth, more from pettiness than from prudence. Yet there is sometimes a slip. An executive secretary may leak a critical fact about a competitor's overtures. An "accidental" happening takes place in which parties are seen discussing corporate destinies. In one famous case, a hotel manager noticed that the board members of two arch-rivals were meeting together for a low-profile luncheon and telephoned the executive offices of one of the firms to verify that the meeting was indeed planned and not accidental. His message, unfortunately, was taken by a secretary other than the intended one. News was out within 30 minutes that a merger was imminent.

Who gets to stay? Can we predict who will survive? One logical answer would be a scenario in which the stronger managers stay and the weaker managers leave. Correct?

Is putting stronger managers into place what most of these cases are all about? Isn't that what stockholders want? It's not that simple. In many cases, strong managers are not easily identified. Definitions of "strong" may vary. Some bankers rate management teams as aggregates, using bottom-line financial results as the main criterion. Other analysts look at individual track records over a career. And the ultimate judges, the owners, may find it difficult to separate individual from group performance. How, for example, is one to interpret a young general manager's potential if his current performance is only marginal? The old owner may have had great faith in the individual for personal reasons or intuitions of the kind developed in hundreds of hours of personal contact and executive grooming. The new owner may have no access to or interest in that kind of history. Investments of this kind may be lost in an instant. They are very hard to discern from the abstract perspective of an acquisition analyst. Yet the beat goes on. Great marriages cannot wait for all the details to be brought to the surface.

Strong managers are those who survive.[3] There are lessons to be learned from this simple truth. When the acquisition is anticipated, it is clear what one must do. The first step is to assess one's survival quotient. Look around the room. Who is most likely to stay? Who has the most clout with the new power structure? Who is the new boss most likely to be? Is one's track record strong enough? If not, is there a godfather or mentor who will intervene to protect?

Safe-bet strategies may come into play. It may be time to develop alternate strategies for surviving the shakeout process. Having a current resume and a copy of *What Color Is Your Parachute?*[4] may be the only alternative.

Followership is the tactic for the majority of individuals involved in a large corporate merger. This entails doing one's job as best one can, watching, and waiting for the next round of changes. Being a good follower may pay off if job security or unchanged employment is the desired result.[5] For many managers, this will be a safe strategy for the tumultuous transition period.

What does this mean? How is one to become a good follower? Some years ago, during one of the authors' consultations with a vice president from a major eastern university, the man said, "We don't need any more leadership programs for the vast majority of our employees. We need something that is not given in these programs. Something that teaches employees to be good employees."

"What do you mean? How so?" were the obvious questions to ask, assuming instantly that this vice president was articulating an authoritarian ego-product. What came back has taken several years and some journeys through traditional training hum-drum to understand.

"Just the simple truths . . . ," he said, "keeping your job, letting your boss know when things are not right, and making sure to keep a positive attitude and loyalty . . . we ought to train this stuff. For God's sake we need it, not a hundred more leaders around here."

Now, years later, this translates into "good follower-ship." Not presuming to know more than one actually knows. Caring. Looking for a chance to put in a good word upwards, not because it scores political points, but because one feels good about the place. One feels lucky to be working for the organization, here and now. Such values, if they can be actually felt and articulated, have kept many an employee in the new company.

A senior co-pilot for (formerly secure and growing) Frontier Airlines is now a classroom flight trainer for Continental Airlines. This change included a 20% pay cut and a serious derailment from what Pete Tierney always wanted to do. Yet Pete has a big house payment and a growing family. He might have thrown it all away. Instead, Pete looked at himself and even harder at the reality of what his postacquisition options were, saw a big bend in the road, and stayed. He still had what he really wanted: Denver, his home and family, a decent airline job, and a new future. He rearranged his life and was able to become a good follower. When it really hits Pete what happened, he feels an instant of loss, a split-second of resentment, and then it all fades. He goes to work now each day feeling strangely different, strangely like he is a survivor of something even bigger than his new employer. For Pete was capable of change, capable of adjustment. His qualities *as a person* in a future leadership role with the new company, Continental, are virtually assured to be among the best that the employer could ask for. For Pete also, this was a strange kind of enriching process.

The inability to learn and adopt followership attitudes and skills may be the ultimate derailment from career and employment. Ironically, this is even true for those with high potential for senior management. On the way up, they must learn how to follow and, ultimately, how to ask others to follow their own leadership.[6]

ORGANIZATIONAL STRUCTURE AND STRUCTURAL CHANGE

What kind of structural changes come about as a result of mergers and acquisitions? In consolidating two organizational structures of similar corporations, we will usually find that there are more people than are needed in the new organization, a condition consultants have referred to as *redundancy*.[7] This condition will become obvious for new corporate decision-makers, and difficult decisions will have to be made. People have to be fired.

Frequently new management will design a new architecture to streamline the organization. During the phasing-in period, we have the classic condition of corporate chaos. Confusion reigns. Positions are redundant, titles are confused, and individuals experience high anxiety, especially in middle-level management. Consultants and audit teams are seen. They are there to aid the new dominant managers in putting together the pieces. Sooner or later, the first announcements are made and the first wave of personnel is displaced. In some instances, managers are given liberal early retirement packages, extended severance bonuses, or paid leaves. Special consulting services are made available when it is believed that certain key individuals may need assistance in getting repackaged or marketed for new job searches. Such consultants have carved out a relatively new area called *outplacement*. Managers are increasingly asking for this service when the pink slip arrives.

New structures are sometimes completely new, with new names for traditional functional positions, new lines of reporting, and different spans of control (a concept referring to the number of reporting individuals or subordinates under a manager). Often the organization structure remains similar after the acquisition or merger, but sometimes a new department or feature is added. Usually a new management audit or control feature, this new structure or function can cause confusion and anxiety, since it may have the purpose of reporting managerial performance data to a remote headquarters entity who is never seen in the flesh but is ever present in daily business dealings. This same headquarters is presumed responsible for the issuing of pink slips and other threatening acts.

When structures collide, the fallout can be devastating. Rumors frequently foreshadow events, and the events themselves can amount to major surgery.[8] In consulting to merger-bound companies, the authors have seen cases in which management staffs of the nondominant partner were almost entirely eliminated. In some of these decisions, the dominant managers are not as concerned with who may be competent (i.e., technically proficient) as with who is loyal or who really understands new management's priorities, or with who fits into the new corporate culture. It must be noted that these are largely subjective decisions.[9] Managers may attempt to make them as rational as possible, but they are ultimately personal and subjective.

Perhaps the most radical clash occurs when organizations with diametrically opposed operating philosophies attempt to mesh. For example, some companies have tall structures with a low span of control. There are many levels and few positions under each manager. There may be a long tradition of clearly defined responsibilities that are monitored with tight controls, and a distrust for managers who go beyond their assigned turf.

If such a company merges with one that has taken a different structural approach, the cultures will clash at many levels, and symptoms will appear in psychological and behavioral areas—anxiety, arguments, confusion, management debates, and devaluation of each other's point of view.[10]

The above form of corporate chaos can be subtle. For example, how could one discern the profound difference in philosophy just by looking at the lines of reporting on the organization chart? Most corporate structures are mixtures of different types, and the clashing takes place in few, but important, places. For example, many high-technology manufacturing companies have tall structures at the top of the company, with just a few executives responsible for all the functional and staff operations, while at the lower levels the style is often flat.

At the shop floor level, many workers will report to the manufacturing supervisors. In such places, there is often a very entrepreneurial do-it-yourself flavor to the workforce, while in larger and more established manufacturing firms (the type that are most active in making acquisitions), the flavor is more traditionally bureaucratic and unions prevail.

The top of the structure of the larger, acquiring firm may be very tall and resemble the high-tech firm, thus yielding an impression of structural similarity, yet the operating philosophies of the two companies may be very dissimilar for the major part of the organizations.

Clashing takes place ultimately in the middle and lower levels, involving the philosophies, norms, values, and attitudes of the two merging cultures, and frequently becomes manifest in debate, behavior, decisions, and policy matters. At its worst, it takes the form of sabotage and overt violence. At the base of these clashes is the inherent dissimilarity in histories and leadership influence. However, it is most often subtle with many causes and effects in the overall process. And that process invariably involves conflict and some kind of resolution.

MORALE AND ATTITUDES: THE LUBRICANT

Climate is like the weather—easy to describe, harder to predict, and almost impossible to change. Both Murphy's Law and Gresham's Law apply:

1. If a drop in morale is at all possible given the corporate situation, history, players, etc., it most likely will occur.

2. Bad news and rumor will drive out any good news in circulation; the worst possible scenario of merger–acquisition news will always be the first rumor, and favorable outcomes will be almost totally discounted!

In some cases, the top managers who are designing the corporate marriage give some thought to climate issues, but usually move through them quickly, believing that their best approach is to remain as proactive as possible and that worrying about organizational climate (or culture clash) can become a tail-wagging-the-dog proposition. In practice, that becomes a task for middle management (or human resource specialists). On the other hand, it is also believed that time will cure any mistrust and that trying to be proactive is not useful. Cynical? Perhaps, but today's action-oriented managers would rather do something than talk or worry about what morale will result. Interestingly, Ed Schein has noted that the entire issue of cultural mesh and resulting climate issues is often performed as a postmerger problem.[11]

In fact, from an observer-analyst point of view, morale can be a major impediment. A recent airline acquisition involved a bid by one company's union to block the deal for months because the employees were so affected by the surprise acquisition announcement after years of "We'll never sell out" messages from senior management.[12] On the other hand, there are cases where the morale factor seems to have been managed proactively. Some companies do much to reassure their ranks that there will be a minimum of damage. In one case, the employees were given at least one vehicle to channel psychological energy in a constructive direction. Sperry and Burroughs (Unisys) offered their employees an incentive to participate in creating the new company name and corporate identification program. Human resource professionals from both companies participated extensively in designing a program to address the infrastructure issues of morale, teamwork, and employee identification. It appears that such proactive efforts pay off in reducing the usual and inevitable difficulties in transition. Unfortunately, the Unisys example is an exception.

CORPORATE CULTURE AND NORMS

As stated earlier, unlike romance and interpersonal attraction, companies come together for chiefly strategic reasons. They do not join because of like cultures. After the merger, cultural integration becomes a requirement for getting under way with the new organization, much like efforts to satisfy the Environmental Protection Agency or paying taxes.

Yet all of the principles of culture development and evolution apply. Cultures do resist changes and sudden shifts in direction. The core elements of organizational icebergs are essentially immutable.

The history of mergers and acquisitions contains many examples of corporate cultures that were resistant to the point of near paralysis. This is particularly true where senior management of the dominant partner is oblivious to the subtle power of middle management and the customs and habits of the nondominant partner. For example, the six-year marriage of Dart & Kraft was terminated after significant frustration from trying to make the merger work. In the words of one analyst, "Nothing in the two companies ever seemed to fit."

When corporate cultures collide, what actually happens? What are the major things to expect? Where do we look for the action?

Analyzing corporate chaos after merger and acquisition is a quasi science. There is expectation and there is disappointment. Carefully planned strategies turn into busted plays on the corporate landscape. The previous discussion helps us form expectations about what to expect *inside* firms after a merger. But how do external forces interact with internal dynamics? And what are the processes that are fueling internal organizational dynamics from outside, where they have a life cycle of their own?

OUTSIDE FORCES

When a company begins an acquisition program, sometimes it starts with only a subconscious idea, usually by the CEO or an active board member. Some idea gets the juices flowing. Usually it is very personal.[13]

Given the personal stakes of merger mania, it is not surprising that the idea begins in someone's fantasy, often at a point where an organization's (or an executive's) life cycle is at a plateau. Sometimes it germinates because the CEO is bored and wants to find a new game to play.

The Study Phase

Then the idea gets rolling. Someone is commissioned to study feasibility, or scenarios of success and failure. The authors, for example, have participated in external consultation contracts where a CEO commissions a highly confidential team to look at competitors as acquisition targets. In one case, we generated 14 unique combinations of business plans and scenarios for the parent company, our client, including scenarios in which the company would acquire, merge, or even become an acquisition target.

When the planning becomes serious, confidentiality becomes paramount. Usually the CEO shares the vision with very few. And sometimes he or she may not be clear in his or her own thinking. More than a few times, consultants have been hired to pursue an elusive target, only to find that half the battle is pinning down the CEO on what he or she really wants. When leaks occur, strategies may be ruined in an instant if a particular gambit is under way. Since many of the gambits actually rely on the element of surprise and timing, and less on proprietary knowledge or executive skill, they require almost perfect sequencing of actions and deft communication with trusted key players (see box).

THE PLANNING THAT LED TO PROFITABLE MERGER OF BANKS

How does a small bank go about doubling its size through a "merger of equals"? On the surface, it's a knotty process. But with computers and a bit of long-range planning and some outside consultants, it's feasible.

Early last year, First National Corp. President Robert Richley compiled a series of detailed computerized models of what kind of bank First National could become.

He then selected more than two dozen "target banks" around the state and "tried to understand how each of them was being managed."

First National executives then whittled the list to a top 10, and held "get together" meetings with officials of each institution. First National did not play all its cards, however, and several of the banks had no idea that the real reason for the meetings was to explore a potential merger.

Richley then reported his findings to First National's board, which decided on the final candidates—

National Bank of La Jolla, National Bank of Fairbanks Ranch and Rancho Santa Fe National Bank.

Meetings with those banks were held in September, an independent consultant was brought in to determine the value of each bank, a tentative agreement was reached in late November, and a definitive agreement was penned just before Christmas.

If all goes according to plan, the deal could close in February or March.

"We wanted a situation where 1 and 1 adds up to 4," said Richley. Two caveats were attached to the negotiations, according to officials. First, there was to be no goodwill or other premium paid by any of the participants.

And, second, once the independent consultants had determined the value of each bank, there could be no negotiations over price.

SOURCE: Bill Ritter, *Los Angeles Times*, 13 January 1987, p. J3. Copyright, 1987, Los Angeles Times. Reprinted by permission.

It should be pointed out that such a planning phase is both formal and informal. It can take as little as several days or as long as a decade.[14] For those on the outside wanting to anticipate deals, one should strive to get close to the planning if at all possible. This could mean accessing data of a privileged nature or testing various hypotheses by direct query or intervention. Rumors have been generated, for example, from reactions of board members or CEOs to direct questions at shareholders' meetings or in press conferences. Many investors pick up tips from a technique of cross-referencing various comments and investigating the resulting hypotheses.[15] Investors are perhaps more sensitive to such information than employees, in that they study such matters in the regular course of business. Employees might discover fateful takeover dramas only after their careers are part of the unfolding scenario itself.

Resistance

One of the inevitable forces when news of an acquisition or merger leaks to the public is some form of resistance. The common forms include:

1. *Subtle resistance and noncompliance*. The fear and anxiety reach levels where employees finally act out their dislikes and worst fantasies, sometimes even far worse than actual facts would dictate. Unfortunately, in this arena constructive logic does not always prevail. Employees see their companies in very personal terms, even in ways they never previously had experienced. The company can become the equivalent of family. When employees sense that their employer will be acquired, new loyalty develops. And it can become quite strong. It is often the loyalty shown the underdog. Employees may react to a takeover in the same fashion as they would react to an attack on a family member.

2. *Overt violence.* Resistance can become extreme. This can take the form of strikes, slowdowns, lockouts, sabotage, white-collar theft, absenteeism, libel, and violence.

3. *Employee buy-backs.* Sometimes employees organize their efforts and combine their blocks of stock ownership to take positions in the postmerger phase. As we have seen, leveraged buyouts have become a common form of this activity.

Waging Psychological War

One important source of corporate chaos is psychological warfare.[16] Once it is established that a target exists, and resistance has shown its face, the management of the would-be dominant partner may choose to conduct an aggressive campaign to win over the various critical interest groups involved in the takeover. All public pronouncements are designed to capture the loyalty, affection, and interest of employees, agents, stockholders, and even government regulators who will eventually be party to the marriage. The best face of the dominant partner is shown.

THE BASIC SCENARIOS

We have identified a few key sources of corporate chaos. A company can acquire, or be acquired. It can merge with another, in a structure of equality and partnership, or it can participate in an unbalanced merger. It can be taken public, or it can be bought out and privatized. Or it can remain in a prolonged state of business and structural limbo, with qualities of complexity and confusion. Finally, it can grow and prosper, or it can fail and enter bankruptcy. These scenarios represent a limited number of outcomes, a limited number of dramas. In an interesting way, all organizations are caught in one of these scenarios, by design or by default. Change may be taking place very slowly and very subtly, or it may be taking place with suddenness and in great public exposure. It is fascinating that the scenarios are this limited in number and, therefore, this simple.

MERGER–ACQUISITION CHAOS: A METHOD TO THE MADNESS?

Are the events described in this chapter predictable? Are they regular enough to enable us to make educated guesses about what may happen next?

Certainly, some companies have pursued acquisitions and encountered many of the same kinds of challenges, such as internal resistance, stockholder backlash, culture clash, and so on. But are the problems occurring at the same points in the cycle? Is there some underlying pattern?

Some experts believe there is.[17] The pattern follows a basic sequence from the initial creation of the game plan through implementation and consolidation. A more or less typical sequence:

1. *Conception stage.* Someone (the chairman of the board, a chief financial officer, or a friend) initiates the basic concept behind a merger or acquisition program. This stage is usually preceded by a long period of corporate seasoning and readiness for the gelling of the ingredients. Some of the ingredients are: an ambitious leader, a business fit in which there is some apparent advantage to combining the forces of two organizations, and a time frame in which the drama should take place in order to be advantageous. Both firms often stand to benefit through the creation of synergy ("one plus one equals three . . . .")

2. *Intelligence/espionage stage.* Some may call this acquisition planning or strategic planning. Data must be gathered. Timing is of the essence. If the companies involved are public and speculation is likely, or if inside information is hot, the planning and surveillance must be done in great secrecy.

3. *Public courtship stage.* Psychological warfare may prevail. Or harmonious partnership may be the nature of interactions. In the case of the recent (1986) Burroughs–Sperry merger described earlier, there was a tone of mutuality, and many were involved from both sides in the joint human resource planning process. When National and Pan American merged into one airline in the late 1970s, there were great

media blitzes proclaiming the harmonious effort to blend the two carriers into one great company. Many National Airlines employees were concerned about a total eclipse of company identity within the merger process, since Pan American was the dominant partner in the merger of staff and assets. Their fears were confirmed when staff positions were consolidated, corporate uniforms were standardized around Pan Am tradition, and operational systems were molded to the Pan Am norms. The courtship can be positive or negative, given the beliefs by each party about what they stand to gain or lose.

4. *Consummation stage*. This occurs when the formal knot is tied. The die is cast for the losing or minority partner, and graceful face-saving behavior is predictable. Announcements are prepared, and the tough decisions begin. Former combatants retire or stop fighting. Deals made earlier are revealed to the rest of the company. At this stage, a vanquished CEO may begin the graceful retirement process, relying mostly on golden parachute packages for a lucrative (albeit humble) departure. The gold watch business booms! Parties and retirement banquets testify to the years of toil.

5. *Honeymoon stage*. Mostly good things happen. New appointments and promotions are made. Promises of synergy and opportunity fill the air. A company logo or new name may be crafted. Stationery, symbols, advertisements, commercials, titles, and products are

renamed or reaffirmed. In theory, the best of both is extracted, tested, and melded. In reality, this may never happen. Even when good intentions are held, the brute force of business reality dominates and forces streamlining. At this point, the honeymoon is over. The majority of employees squirm and wince as the fallout begins. Rumors abound. Corporate chaos has begun.

A MODEL

A picture says a thousand words. A model tells what is behind a thousand pictures. In the following pages, we shall attempt to lay out the basic structure of merger-acquisition dynamics and depict the patterns of corporate chaos.

The model is based on a systems approach with inputs, internal processes (sometimes called through-puts), outputs, and stages within each sector of flow. One may think of it as if there are causes of multiple origin and many, many resulting effects. The details are unique in each corporation, but the basic event-flow is the same. Events enter the arena (inputs), they cause things to happen inside the company (internal throughputs), and they cause both planned and unplanned results (outputs). These can help or hinder corporate functioning and individual success and security on the job. The processes are interrelated. And the cycles start new cycles, and the whole flow starts all over again.

Now for some of the details. Consider these events in a typical scenario of acquisition:

1. A CEO conceives of the idea. A target is identified.

2. Acquisition planning is begun. Espionage and careful study of the candidate company are commissioned and carried out by consultants.

3. Word leaks out. Psychological warfare is triggered. Announcements are made about intentions. Third parties are contracted, and large blocks of stock ownership are traded. Greenmail appears and ownership begins to shift.

4. Tender offers are made. One big one is accepted.

5. Pep rallies and parties are thrown.

6. Subterfuge begins. Some employees threaten to block the orderly process of acquisition.

7. Layoffs and staff reductions (downsizing) begin.

8. Restructuring takes place.

9. Subsidiaries are sold and/or closed down. Several new ones are started.

10. The company takes on a new name and moves its corporate headquarters to the West Coast.

11. Stock prices stabilize.

12. The new company announces new products and prepares for its next spurt of growth.

13. Four years hence it is acquired by a Japanese conglomerate.

The cycles repeat. Memories are short, because much energy and stress are expended in the heat of battle.

In almost every case, an autopsy would reveal a similar structure to the drama. There are winners. There are losers. And some of the losers this time will be winners in the next round!

PERCEIVING CHAOS AT THE TIP OF THE ICEBERG

The iceberg theory indicates that we only see the barest surface detail of the whole story. We could go on and on in describing every bit of corporate behavior in infinitesimal detail. But how boring! Our challenge is to be efficient! We wish to describe the essence of the whole story in just a quick but accurate analysis. We strive to get to the core of the matter as quickly as we can, sometimes also as secretly as we can.

After all, a skilled observer need not view every aspect of the organization in order to make informed guesses about where the firm is heading. Good hunches make the adrenalin flow. Accurate ones may make the bank account bulge.

Now apply this to the model. Apply the law of icebergs to the fact that we are able to get only a subjective, random sample of corporate behavior at a given moment. Perhaps we are reading a preprogrammed piece of corporate propaganda, such as a prospectus for buying stock. Now what happens?

Chances are, we have gaps in the information. There are missing pieces in the emerging organizational mosaic. Chunks of the iceberg are missing or, more likely, below the surface. In realistic terms, this usually means that we cannot see *all* of what is happening. Maybe there is a subtle employee backlash in motion, but it is hidden behind a facade of public communication. Or maybe it just has not yet had a good chance to come to the surface.

Perhaps someone is manipulating a piece of the expected system-cycle. Maybe a step has been suppressed or disguised. Maybe the employee shock and adjustment is too ugly and is blanketed by an employee involvement in the new company name contest, or in a change of headquarters from one city to another. And sometimes such moves can actually help.

Roles, structures, and historical corporate boundaries all change in a big merger. This metamorphosis takes time and consumes vast amounts of human energy and emotion. No single person has the vantage point from which this can all be taken in. No one can feel all the emotions. No individual can imagine all the different impacts.

SO NEAR TO HOME

The suddenness with which merger and acquisition can change the lives and attitudes of people is literally astounding. While attending a "Buy US Saving Bonds" luncheon for CEOs recently in a major West Coast city, the president of a major, just-acquired financial institution expressed himself candidly when asked by some friends if he would be remaining with the company. The parent corporation had its headquarters in New York. He said with poignant frankness that he honestly had no idea where he would be going. While the parent company has a practice of treating their employees very well, he pointed out that it firmly believes in the principle of unitary command—one boss! This meant that he would be displaced. Not because he had poor job performance (he had been in the CEO role exactly 18 months and had produced excellent financial performance), but because he was now in a one-down position. Here was a $225,000 per year executive with four school-age children, recently moved from Atlanta to the West, out of a job at the age of 47. Not sure of his exact title, he would be on the market in 30 days. Many of the thousands of rank-and-file employees in his company could not imagine, literally could not believe, this reality—their president, almost out of a job!

In fact, the suddenness with which such key executives are displaced has left many questioning whether there is some foul play involved. For example, if executives in key, pivotal roles can engineer the acquisition of competitors silently and craftily, they can also surely engineer the process in reverse. Suppose, for example, that this man had a double mission. He was hired to help a struggling company keep standing amid the fray. Yet, secretly, even subconsciously, he could be an agent for the acquiring competitor. All of his efforts would be in disguise. Carefully acting his way through the boardroom dramas, he positions the struggling firm at the brink, and while it teeters, he steps back to be part of its fall. Either a golden parachute becomes his reward, or reemployment within the industry, somewhere in the complex maze of executive talent that sooner rather than later becomes lost in the shuffle. Far fetched? Many stockholders and government officials are wondering if such scenarios are currently embedded in our contemporary list of who's who.

SURVIVING CORPORATE CHAOS

Which leads us to the dilemma of how to survive and make progress in these important and inevitable human endeavors. How should we counsel individual human beings through the buffeting of these inhumane transitions? How are we to understand the human responses and make sense from the nonsense? How are we to navigate amid icebergs?

EXECUTIVE SUMMARY

- This chapter outlines the ways in which merger and corporate chaos impact corporate functioning. When companies marry and divorce, their symbolic and physical sides pass through shock and trauma, sometimes resulting in complete obliteration of the great and unique features that are part of tradition.

- Resistance takes a heavy toll. Impact on productivity, morale, and teamwork are the obvious costs, but there is a silent rage that is equally devastating. The scenarios can be anticipated in a pending merger.

ENDNOTES

1. See Bennis, Warren and Nanus, Bert, *Leaders* (New York: Harper and Row, 1985) for a good survey of leadership style and patterns in contemporary corporations.
2. See Leighton, Charles and Tod, Robert, "After the Acquisition: Continuing Challenge," *Harvard Business Review*, March–April 1969, p. 90.
3. For a good analysis of survival styles of management, see Michael Maccoby's *The Gamesman* (New York: Simon & Schuster, 1976).
4. This book by Richard Bolles is a classic work on the subject of reemployment and career change. (Berkeley: Ten Speed Press, 1979).
5. See Smith, Roy, "How to Be a Good Subordinate," *USAir Magazine*, January 1982, p. 39.
6. See McCall and Lombardo, "What Makes a Top Executive?," *Psychology Today*, February 1983, pp. 26, 28–31.
7. See Bolman, Lee and Deal, Terrence, *Modern Approaches to Understanding and Managing Organizations* (San Fran-

cisco: Jossey-Bass, 1984) for excellent discussion of types of industrial organization and accompanying management styles.

8. Broder, John, "B of A Battle: Classic Case of Psychological Warfare," *Los Angeles Times*, January 1987, IV, p. 1.

9. See Magnet, Myron, "Acquiring without Smothering," *Fortune*, 12 November 1984, p. 22, for effective counterpoint.

10. See Harris, Philip, *Management in Transition* (San Francisco: Jossey-Bass, 1985) and Harris' *New World, New Ways, New Management* (New York: AMACOM, 1983) for discussion of trends in transitional structure and new approaches to combining differing structures.

11. Schein, Edgar, *Organizational Culture and Leadership* (San Francisco: Jossey-Bass, 1985), pp. 34–36.

12. "Merger Rumor Untrue, PSA Tells Employees," *San Diego Tribune*, 22 October 1986, p. A-21.

13. One of the best examples is the story behind Armand Hammer's long desire to own the "Arm & Hammer" baking soda company Church & Dwight. See Donald Woutat's "Oxy's Hammer, Arm & Hammer Go Arm in Arm," *Los Angeles Times*, 23 September 1986, CC/IV.

14. In the recent case of USAir's bid to acquire Pacific Southwest Airline (PSA), USAir Chairman Ed Colodny said that he and USAir have been looking at PSA for the past ten years. *San Diego Tribune*, 12 December 1986, p. AA-1.

15. Budde, Neil, "How to Find, Speculate on Hot Takeover Rumors," *USA Today*, 3 November 1986, p. 3B.

16. Many contemporary references abound in current media and periodicals. The recent Bank of America–First Interstate Bank takeover battle is a prime example. See Sing, Bill and Furlong, Tom, "BankAmerica, 1st Interstate Merger Seen Leading to Cuts in Staff and Branch Closings," *Los Angeles Times*, 8 October 1986, CC/IV.
17. See Lawrence, John, "In Takeovers, Human Toll Is Often Ignored," *Los Angeles Times*, 14 December 1986, IV.

8

IMPACT: THE HUMAN DIMENSION

This chapter identifies and analyzes certain key psychological processes resulting from corporate chaos. This is where corporate destiny and human destiny come together, perhaps where they clash.

Pessimism and optimism are powerful forces. Any corporation experiencing significant change will inevitably evoke these emotions. The ability of managers to deal with these forces may determine the ultimate success or failure of the firm. Employees who participate in the change process may gain a great deal of relief from the anxiety and stress we have described earlier if understanding, insight, and goodwill are forthcoming from senior managers. Easier said than done! And for good reason.

The literature is full of cases in which the psychological effect from mergers or acquisitions was devastating. Researchers have found that morale of employees in both corporations typically becomes damaged after takeovers.[1] Changes in organizational structure can drastically alter the quality of work life for many employees and can hit minorities especially hard.[2] Even before resorting to merger and acquisition, managers typically feel the pinch and begin to shut operations down.[3] Productivity and morale may be diminished as a result. How can we begin to understand and grapple with the dynamics involved here?

ON THE LIMITS OF POWER

The fact that the business media has hyped the corporate restructuring movement of the last decade is not surprising. But the fact that it smacks of psychopathology *is* significant. The problems are real, they are well documented, and they reach into almost every industry and sector.

The human emotions resulting from corporate chaos must be clearly understood. Though they are, of course, subjective in nature, we must make an attempt to understand them objectively.[4] Here are some of their most usual forms when crisis, stress, or tragedy strike.

1. *Confusion*. Rumors may start the process and chaos develops. No one knows quite what to believe.

2. *Frustration*. One's job, career, or investment appears to be in clear jeopardy. Efforts to help are met with resistance.

3. *Anger*. Tempers flare; conflict begins. People are angry and may show it.

4. *Subterfuge/sabotage*. A stronger reaction than anger. Direct revenge is acted out. Someone gets hurt and there are losses.

5. *Alienation/burnout/defeat*. One is too discouraged and tired to fight. There is a sense of powerlessness.

These stages, like those described by Kubler Ross in her research on the human reactions to death and dying, are almost predictable. Yet we need to understand more profoundly the psychology of powerlessness.

ISSUES FOR THE INDIVIDUAL

Those involved as employees are affected in various ways when merger and acquisition take place. The case study literature is full of situations in which unintended consequences amounted to great loss, destruction, and wasted resources for some organizations,[5] including some of the largest and most well known American corporations.

On the human side, these are difficult times. Shock is followed by actual loss. Families are displaced. Careers are uprooted, and hard decisions must be made. Individuals who have power in the corporation may find their power challenged and taken away.

Even the brightest find that they cannot predict the next day's events. Corporate forces are bigger than anyone's personal sphere of influence. Even presidents are fired in hostile takeovers.

Some realize their powerlessness. Many fight the idea. A few are able to triumph over it. So what does this mean? Philosophically it means that it is healthiest to accept that this may happen to you. If it does, moving on and growing are essential. Fighting and frustration are inevitable in the short term, but there comes a time to accept what one cannot change. Worse yet, perhaps, are those cases in which there is the illusion of control. These are the situations in which managers might actually think that they have accounted for the complex changes and impacts or feel that they are under control, when actually they are not.[6]

THE ROLE OF PERCEPTION: HALF-EMPTY OR HALF-FULL?

How we perceive can make all the difference. For example, one can view job displacement as ruin or as growth and learning. Corporations provide the basic necessities for most employees:

¶ Employment
¶ Social networks, friends, colleagues
¶ Learning and professional growth

Yet after merger and acquisition, the great moments are often forgotten, and bad news prevails. Some people stay burned out and depressed for years, and a few never make it back.

And then there are the optimists. The hardy few who lead others and themselves out of the ashes. They see the same events and react differently. They see opportunity in every change. They need to see the world as correctable and liveable, in spite of the diversity. The glass is still half-full.

HOW PARANOIA IMPACTS PERCEPTION

An interesting phenomenon occurs when we have individuals in companies who are under extreme stress and yet who have an active sense of optimism and fantasy. These are people who, when they experience events that are consistent with their beliefs and hopes, literally perceive that organizations are acting on their own, beyond people, beyond leaders. Paranoia accounts for seeing the company as a machine out of control. These phenomena have been called "thingified abstractions" by University of Oregon Professor Emeritus Dwaine Richins. Innocent as they may be at the time (e.g., "The company is giving less money to charitable causes this year"), they can sometimes take on Orwellian proportions, e.g., "The company will determine my entire career in the future."

It should be pointed out that thingified abstractions are exaggerations and sometimes hysterical in nature. They can cast one's whole thinking into an implicitly passive style. Companies do not determine, except *in perception*, an individual's career path. Rather, individual superiors and bosses (other people) do!

One of the most prevalent types of mind-artifacts impacting individuals in corporate culture is the much-discussed phenomenon of *institutional fiction*. Simply stated, when individuals believe that a given company, corporation, or group is actually more than the immediate and present participants, they have made the jump to seeing the company as having a total sphere or force of great proportions. The larger-than-life quality of corporations is fed by the emotional needs of participants to confirm their emotional reality, which may indeed be greatly engaged at the moment by their involvement with the organization. Giving it fictitious or greatly symbolic (sometimes by metaphor) power confirms one's own sense of powerlessness over the collective reality. Corporate history, for example, takes on immensely powerful meaning. Churches, particularly some of the long-established ones, are good examples. The congregation's perceived meaning of the church at a given moment suggests that its institutional character is the sum of its history *along with* its current state. Its participants are seen as *more than those* at a current gathering. Individuals can feel a real sense of immediacy and nearness with all who have come before in that place *as if they were present at the moment*. Such thinking is sometimes the essence of how those organizations survive. Such believing fosters perceptions by the whole that go beyond the objective facts and happenings of the present. Such forces move individuals and whole communities, and confer a power beyond that rooted in the organization itself.

The role of rumor and informal leaders can greatly feed collective movements of this type. We have seen such powerful forces operate when there is talk of plant closings or, more specifically, when merger and acquisition are in the wind. Hopes and fears abound. Particularly sensitive people may begin to believe that cultural themes or scripts from past history will somehow operate mysteriously to save the company from trouble or disaster. Mythical heroes and scenarios are called upon from memory or fantasy and are sometimes articulated. Union leaders feel and hear some of these when trying to console constituencies in times of great trouble.

WISHFUL THINKING

Such forces can actually create interesting new behavior in the company culture. Instant or overnight heroes are created. Past leaders are resurrected, even posthumously, and sent into battle with the real adversary of the present dilemma. Perceptions of leaders tell us much about how the hopeful mind can work in merger time.

Such happening could be termed *leadership fiction.* It works in the following way. In a circumstance of extreme hardship, sensitive individuals who feel threatened may perceive and believe deeply that "the boss knows me." There is a belief, not just a hope or a wish, that a guardian leader exists and will protect and understand. Many go through their long work lives actually believing that the president of the company knows them, and even likes them. Often they believe that they know and also are fond of the president. This is a real phenomenon, with real consequences. It may, sadly, have no grounding in fact upon objective investigation.

The reality from the authors' years of consulting and research is that presidents rarely know what is going on more than three organizational layers below them! The clerk, in fact, knows the president and *believes* the acquaintance is mutual. Point of fact: The president knows none of the clerks by name, by family, or by aspirations. Yet such unilateral fantasy friendships are the very stuff that makes for all the feeling, the love, the faith, and the goodwill within some companies. It is a many-splendored misperception. It binds and bonds like a glue. In times of great stress, such cultural bonds can give great relief.

CORPORATE HYSTERIA: ICEBERG THEORY

In Chapter 2, it was suggested that mergers and acquisitions are planned for business reasons, not for psychological ones. Yet most of what the public, investors, and employees see are the psychological issues that trigger emotion. The question is: Do you really understand the motivations behind the merger or acquisition?

Thus, we return to our notion of saliency. Our perceptions are driven by the saliency factors. The merger or acquisition is driven by business decisions that are sometimes cold and impersonal and that may be opposed to life as valued by some of the individuals in the respective companies. In a very remote perspective, that taken by Wall Street analysts and investors, there is no right or wrong, there are only smart decisions. Human life in the small town where the plant may be shut down, or where the employees must relocate or take a pay cut, matters not. It cannot. Good business decisions never have valued human impact costs in a terribly serious way. And when such decisions strike close to home, they turn the tables on values.

Maybe we should never invest in our own hometown. One investor's grandparents had all their investment and all of the family's fortune tied to common stock of the hometown company, one of the old heavy industry firms. Emotion prevailed. Loyalty was the thing. Invest in America! Buy bonds! Buy XYZ stock! Thirty years later, nothing was left.

Yet is nothing sacred? How can we really expect to be anything but loyal and invest in our own country, our own hometown, even our own employer? The proviso is, not blindly, and not necessarily forever. It is paramount in today's chaotic corporate environment, with destinies being played out by the power players, the CEOs and insiders who know and may control the big moves, to remember our ancestors, to be smart enough to move our family investments and our careers if we happen, *through no direct fault or cause of our own*, to be caught in one of the unfortunate scenarios.

THE ROLE OF STRESS

A merger or acquisition changes the normal routine. Undoubtedly, this change produces stress, and stress is both a curse and an enigma. It can seriously cripple and throw negativity into an otherwise good work relationship. And it can produce, strangely, a break with negative reality. In its lesser known role, corporate chaos stress can be the gateway to personal recovery.

THE ROLE OF OPTIMISM: A WAY OUT

All of the foregoing is true. All the human frailties apply. Merger, acquisition, and other forms of sudden restructuring all shake up the individual human psyche, emotions, relationships, and loyalties and create other forms of disruption. But there is a silver lining. There are structures and human approaches that heal, preserve, and make it possible to get on with life. These are divided into, first, the things individuals can do to cope better, second, the approaches that managers can take to help others, and last, the approaches that are taken by outside third parties.

Some would argue that it is even possible to *decide* to be happy, to consciously conclude that one will make the best of it, get on with it, and carry an aura of positive energy.[7]

Healing Thyself First

Facing stress and crisis, and what we have called the worst of corporate chaos, individuals can react primarily in one of three modes. These modes reflect the individual's basic values.

1. MODE ONE: Things will get worse.
2. MODE TWO: Things will remain the same; I have time to consider alternatives. I will wait.
3. MODE THREE: Things will get better or I will get better!

Individuals who live in MODE TWO may move on to MODE THREE in time. But MODE THREE is the key to individual coping, surviving, living, and growing.

Getting into MODE THREE is easier said than done. Some people seem to be born optimists. Some learn that this is the only way to live. Still others take up the philosophy in the belief *that there is no other way.* What does this mean?

Bad things do happen. Mergers are bigger than many of us can comprehend. Sometimes we get involved as innocent bystanders or beneficiaries, but most of the time very few get that close to the big picture. Thus, we are usually left with only a *partial* understanding of what, why, and who. We either accept that conclusion, or we fight it, in which case we may be stuck in MODE ONE or MODE TWO. The difficult nut to crack, it would seem, is accepting that fact. Accepting that we have been dealt a bad hand. Or maybe a good hand, but we just can't see it yet. It is not consistent with much of our cultural learning and institutional conditioning to feel powerless and not become frustrated. Working our way up the ladder and getting derailed just doesn't seem fair. But what are we taking for granted? What have we sacrificed for this kind of perfectionism? Much indeed.

Those who live by MODE THREE may implicitly accept that the rules of the game are not comprehensible in the first place. Yet, on closer scrutiny, optimists believe some other things. Life sometimes is not fair, or meant to be easily understood. Tough times are good for testing.

Career changes were somehow meant to be. We are meant somehow to change. There is something awaiting us for which all this difficulty was meant to be training. There is something in addition to me that is running my career, my company, my business, my life. And I must go with that. Not fight it now.

The "Survivor" Mentality.   These individuals can make a change and move on. The stress and chaos are setbacks, not roadblocks. The situation brings out the survivor in the person, and the most difficult situation can become a game, a tolerable challenge. Mike Maccoby describes this breed of survivor, the gamesman, in his research on corporate executives who have this quality of resilience.[8] And the attitudes may be learnable if the individual has mentors and an open mind.

"Getting on with it" takes different forms. But constructive responses involve recovering from job/corporate chaos through the making of proactive, self-directed changes. Many get started and inspired by reading and learning from others, or by making major changes in career direction. Many change occupations entirely. Some find that they are really free of the powerlessness when they can truthfully and selflessly help others with the same problems.

But there is another force for optimism, other than just personal philosophy and attitude. This other factor, a most special force where it occurs, may make all the difference.

The Role of Special People: Corporate Triage

When corporate chaos hits, informal leaders emerge. Some of these are the unsung heroes, those who go to lengthy ends to help and provide spirit in times of dismay and utter confusion. "Who was that masked man?" they ask. Who are these people?

In every crowd, there is nearly always an informal leader, someone to whom a most special kind of leadership is given. These people are not usually the managers or formal authority figures. They will be those who put oil on the waters of pain and conflict between people. They will be those who lead in short time frames—events in which someone needs special human help outside of the line of normal events and corporate affairs. Someone may be dying of cancer, and the spiritual leader becomes his special friend. Or, when acquisition restructuring takes away the spirit from a company, a long-time employee leads a company team to a championship—but quietly and with grace. And as people talk, flutter, and worry about the dissemination of pink slips, an unknown person encourages people to look in the right places for new opportunities—and no one ever asks him or her to do so.

Frequently these employees are motivated by a desire to be helpful and a natural manner for giving what is needed without fanfare. Often they are managers, though they may be at the lowest level of the organization and relative unknowns. They are not charlatans, and they do not have superficial charisma. Their leadership doesn't come from a textbook on situational management, nor does it come from a management development course. It seems to come from elsewhere, perhaps from their earliest character formation.

We have observed and interviewed such heroes in various corporate studies on restructuring. They have been described as modern managers, great facilitators, or highly versatile human beings. They have appeared in the recent literature on excellence in organizations.[9] We usually find them standing at the center of chaos itself. We choose to call this type the spiritual leader. Some might call these special people corporate heroes. They never receive the conventional rewards or recognition. Often they fade into the background and are never seen again. The following characteristics have been identified:

1. They do not care for the limelight; in fact, they seem to stay in the background and shun any public credits.

2. They have developed a following, and a genuine folk hero mythology has grown around their deeds and identity.

3. Their efforts are *for* people, and for causes that help people.

4. They have great skills as listeners; they are better listeners than speakers.

5. They say what comes naturally. In the Asian sense of "KI," their actions and words have a natural, un-rehearsed flow and are appropriate, even powerful, in the episode in which they are a leadership figure.

6. They go far beyond the call of duty.

7. Frequently their deeds are anonymous. Only the person being helped knows of the effort that is given. Sometimes, no one knows except the doer of the deed. But it is always humane, and it is always helpful in nature.

Managers and even senior corporate leaders often perform valiant deeds of leadership. But the quintessential difference here is that they are expected to. It is when the unrecognized rise to the occasion with the brilliance and valiance of a superhero that we see the quality of inspiration described above.

Are such traits and skills learnable? Not entirely. We can study the circumstances for the nuances. We can train ourselves and our students in methods and attitudes of service and leadership. But duplication of the spontaneous qualities seems difficult at best.

The Role of Outside Parties: The Silver Lining?

An entire professional field exists that would purport to help the situation we have labeled corporate chaos. Consultants and senior managers have utilized professionals in this field to help align corporate culture and character after merger and acquisition.

Organizational development (OD) is a professional field that assists organizations in trouble. Trained professionals work with senior management in addressing the postmerger problems affecting people. What do these programs, or interventions, look like?

¶ Corporate information programs to address initial anxiety, confusion, public reactions, etc.

¶ Outplacement services for retired and forced-retirement executives. These services include counseling, job search, career rebuilding, and personal growth experiences.

¶ Team-building workshops and sessions for new corporate groups and units that are pulled together.

¶ Special training programs for new organizational units after restructuring.

¶   Executive counseling for strategic planning of new corporate human resources and personnel policies.

In their 1987 merger, Sperry and Burroughs found that a postmerger success meant high employee involvement in finding and adapting to a completely new corporate name, logo, and corporate identification program. Unisys ("One system") was the result. The teamwork process and culture of organizational development (OD) was heavily used.

Caution: The Placebo.   There are times when using organizational development services can mask or tranquilize an organization's true destiny. It can be used as a pill or placebo—something to divert attention from the true nature of intentions and outcomes.

Some years ago, we were retained as consultants to a large plastics manufacturer in New Jersey. The general manager wanted an improved training program and said that he really needed more teamwork and cooperation in the plant. A program of organizational development activities was proposed, and shortly after the initial discussions a three-month schedule of team building, role clarification, job-enrichment training, quality circles, and supervisory retreats began.

In the early weeks of the program, the consultants and corporate employees got under way. A new aura of excitement and enthusiasm seemed to sweep over the entire company. One day, however, a disgruntled salesman pulled one of the consultants aside. The man took the consultant to a conference room in an adjoining company building, where he introduced him to the team leader of the Big Eight accounting firm's junior audit team. Only one question was needed to put all in sharp focus. It was the question of the day! "What is all this?"

The answer: The English company that was buying the plastics firm was conducting a preacquisition audit of inventory and accounts of sales. It seems there were some irregularities or, at least, some questions.

Do you, the reader, see what was going on? It was curious that the general manager mentioned nothing of the pending corporate acquisition. And it was no accident that none of the employees knew the real story until that moment! The organizational development program turned sour. The program had been used to divert attention from what surely would have been the usual subterfuge and drop in morale following announcement of the acquisition. In this case, management knew that disgruntled employees, fearing the worst about acquisition by a foreign firm, may have blown cover and revealed that the books had been salted. The general manager took the risk, and instead he had a near employee riot plus an IRS investigative team to deal with. Even the consultants were fooled.

The consulting lore abounds with such true stories of misuse, abuse, and malfeasance in dealing with the collective interests and emotions of real employees. Many of the stories involve well-meaning professionals who might have been tricked or just might not have been thorough enough on the front end of a project. They go on and learn from these experiences. And employees would do well to scrutinize such activities, not because it is better to be cynical, but because some of these programs are neither real nor true. The other shoe doesn't always drop. But look to see if there is another shoe about to fall.

ON THE NATURE OF CORPORATE DESTINY: THE ENIGMA

We have used the concept of *corporate destiny* throughout this book. Understanding future trends and environmental patterns, such as depicted in the highly acclaimed book *Megatrends*[10] by John Naisbitt, is useful as a context for a specific corporation's path into the future, but it only gives clues. Corporate destiny refers to the future state of a corporation, but the future state anticipated to follow one of a limited number of paths. And we can at least think about that in advance and know that with certainty a future course is at this moment in process (by default), perhaps, even, in someone's conscious planning process. We understand and believe this concept to be among the simplest but most profound in employee and managerial minds. We can only know and appreciate the exact details of that destiny after it has actually begun to play out.

Yet there is a series of paradoxes and riddles here. Consider your corporation at this moment. It has a history, if only brief, perhaps. And it exists now, at this moment. And it will exist in some form, with some strategic direction in the future. The future may simply mean tomorrow morning! But tomorrow morning you may arrive at work to find the company has moved, changed, been bought, or has bought another!

That state, subtly different or dramatically changed, is its destiny, as we understand and describe it today. It is tomorrow's company on today's market. It is the company of tomorrow, defined—or planned—today!

And this has different value for managers than it may for employees. It has significant meaning for investors, because it is the very essence of why they are involved in the first place. It has very different meaning for those who passively, or helplessly, react to events than it does for those who act on events. There are keepers of the secrets of corporate destiny. And there are those who cannot possibly know. And there are some who would rather not be in the arena of destiny forces, those who want to remain uninvolved.

It is an inherently exciting idea. Like death. It awaits all. No one escapes destiny. And it shapes our lives, for better or for worse. Companies can transform, marry, divorce, die, be reborn, and they can grow to be giants. Their destinies and ours intertwine. Some people actually control company destinies. The majority are controlled *by* them.

The riddle is that we are free agents and given to choosing our own destiny. But we may be pawns in larger games and schemes. And in today's high-tech world of financial decision-making, even computers are players!

Our best educated and most charismatic executives can become transformed overnight, from control and power brokers to passive riders on golden parachutes. From giants and mavericks to puppets and pawns. Destiny will prevail, whatever it is. There will always be some eventuality ahead—some form of corporate destiny. You cannot stop it from taking some course. You cannot freeze a company, or its culture, or its people, or its owners, or its subtle, powerful forces within. Maybe the grandest enigma of all, and frankly half our human fun, is that we sometimes think we can.

Freeze today's vision of tomorrow's company. Hold it for a moment in your mind. Invest money in it. Invest yourself there. Now, blink, step back, look again. Didn't you know it would be different than what you saw? How different? That element will make or break your fortune, maybe your career. Come close, and you will be a winner and, for this round, a successful player of destiny!

EXECUTIVE SUMMARY

- Making a merger or acquisition work takes more than a clever strategy. Managing the human dimension is critical.

- Human emotions after a merger or acquisition take differing forms, from confusion to alienation and burnout.
- The role of philosophy is critical: The glass can be viewed as half-empty or half-full.
- Informal leaders facilitate the coping process.
- The role of personal philosophy (survivor mentality) is critical for both partners in a merger.

ENDNOTES

1. DeMeuse, Kenneth, research reported by Intergraph, Huntsville, Alabama, in Fisher, Kathleen, "Company Raids Shatter Morale," *APA Monitor*, October 1986, p. 32.
2. Ciabattari, Jane, "When Change Is in the Wind . . . HEADS UP!" *Working Woman*, February 1987.
3. Carmichael, Dan, "Merger Mania Causing Managers to Worry about Own Job Security," *San Diego Daily Transcript*, 19 November 1986.
4. Marks, Mitchell and Mirvis, Philip, "Merger Syndrome: Stress and Uncertainty," *Mergers and Acquisitions*, Summer 1985, p. 52.
5. "Corporate Raider Goldsmith Leaves Goodyear in Shambles," *San Diego Union*, 30 November 1986, p. I–7.
6. For a good discussion of self-defeating psychology in postmerger stress, see Mirvis, Philip and Marks, Mitchell,

"Merger Syndrome: Management by Crisis," *Mergers and Acquisitions*, January–February 1986, pp. 70–76.

7. See Greenwald, Harold and Rich, Elizabeth, *The Happy Person* (New York: Avon, 1984).
8. Maccoby, Michael, *The Gamesman* (New York: Simon & Schuster, 1976).
9. See Peters, Thomas and Waterman, Robert, *In Search of Excellence* (New York: Harper and Row, 1981), p. 83.
10. Naisbitt, John, *Megatrends* (New York: Warner Books, 1982).

9

IS THERE LIFE AFTER MERGER MANIA?

Social systems, such as corporations, are interconnected. Disturbances in their equilibrium by reorganization or merger impact all the stakeholders in that enterprise and have a ripple effect. That is, other entities connected to that institution may be impacted by the change—such as their suppliers and customers, other companies in their industry, or any activities of an interdependent nature. The elimination of a department, or a plant, or a product line as a result of an acquisition, for instance, may have adverse effects upon a town's economic health, a local government's budget, and the sales of allied products and services in the vicinity.

The decade of the 1980s has seen the rise of merger mania and deal-making. Much of the literature on mergers in America centers on financial and purely economic impacts.[1] Some are questioning even whether the entire phenomenon of "merger mania" is beneficial or highly destructive to the economy overall.[2] Little has actually been written about the larger significance to our social and management systems and particularly the human impact. The net effect is that corporate chaos has resulted, leaving some in riches, some in great loss of job, career, or fortune. Corporations do have destinies, and some of them are bound to survive, but others will not. Yet what does all of this mean? Where are we headed?

This chapter attempts to summarize our findings and conclusions. Before concluding that the tone is pessimistic, remember that we live in a society in which we are always at risk. We do not strive for cradle-to-grave security. Part of the American ethic is to take a chance, to attempt to win, to try one's luck, and to invest hard work for the privilege of being able to retire in comfort.[3] Keep this in mind as we analyze the nature of life after merger mania.

For starters, it is important to point to the significance of patterns in an overall "big picture" sense. And there are some big patterns afoot.

POINT-COUNTERPOINT: REASONS FOR PESSIMISM?

Poised at one extreme is the notion and challenge of the "casino economy," discussed so well by James Fallows in his original article in *Atlantic Monthly*. This view holds that a significant portion of GNP is really artificial, a product of corporate valuation fueled by the "betting" syndromes, such as merger rumors. At the other extreme is the view that we are witnessing the beginning glimpses of a new and streamlined American corporation, a sort of fortress corporate America, emerging through the merger wars.[4] What we really have here are two positions or vantage points from which merger mania can be viewed: an economy fueled by artificial forces versus an economy in which a phoenix-like new form is emerging. If the former is mostly true, we have inflated value and a house of cards. If the latter is more accurate, we have an exciting era just ahead, one in which we are looking at *the full value economy* for the first time.

Sony's Morita has put the challenge in another way. In his recent analysis of what is right and wrong with the American economy in global markets, he has concluded that American managers are entirely too short-term-oriented.[5] Managerial performance is rewarded on the basis of short-term gains and cost reduction, rarely for creativity or long-term thinking. The usual time frame of reference for managerial assessment and reward is semi-annually to annually. Yet part of the difficulty lies in the very nature of managerial assessment. Pressures are real, and they are felt in short-term cycles. Opportunities for demonstrating performance, especially the dramatic kind that gets big bonuses, are more short than long term in nature. The emergence of the newly minted MBA who makes a million dollars on Wall Street during the first five years of his career has done nothing to make managers more patient.

Much of merger mania and resulting corporate chaos deals with rapid-fire moves and quick turnaround of poor performance. The incentive for making it "right

the first time" or "making real things well" over time, as
Morita has challenged, is just not there.

REASONS FOR CONCERN

Let us look further. What other evidence do we see to
support a conclusion that there is something flawed and
false about the prosperity of the last decade? What else
portends lurking danger within the corporate moves of
merger mania? The last quarter of 1986 and early 1987,
for example, saw the rise of another major pattern—
"scandal mania" and insider trading. More than one
major investment banking institution and prominent
leaders of that industry were cited for insider trading.
Federal authorities from the SEC and FBI undertook
lengthy investigations that promised to ferret others out
of the Wall Street woodwork before this round was
complete.

These individuals, until they are arrested, wield
huge amounts of power. In a world in which power is
money and money "talks," these individuals can manip-
ulate major corporations. But, of course, so can the law-
abiding raiders and heavy hitters in the merger–acquisition game. Bill Creson, former president of Crown
Zellerbach, points out that stockholders and boards are
being asked to make decisions affecting the entire destinies of good, well-established corporations within a few

weeks of the time that the raiders move in. Such power and influence are difficult for individual groups of stockholders, or employees and their unions, to deal with. It has been pointed out that there is more than just financial value to the make-up of a corporation.[6]

RESTRUCTURING CAN BE POSITIVE

Many of the raiders will be quoted as saying that their moves are really in stockholders' best interests.[7] They state frequently that they fully intend to restructure the company, make it leaner and meaner, and fire incompetent management. Such moves to cut out the fat of bureaucracy are sometimes welcomed by stockholders and even employees. In our analysis, though, restructuring can be both beneficial and harmful. On the one hand, the potential benefits are clear. Case after case provides illumination. Restructuring, cutting out unprofitable units, and firing redundant layers of personnel can provide the only path to survival for firms in highly competitive industries.[8]

Unfortunately, the restructuring is sometimes just cosmetic. Or, worse yet, it is done because there is a ceremonial or *expected* need to do so. There may be an automatic and self-fulfilling agenda to *do something* in the aftermath of a merger or acquisition. The public pressure for presenting "evidence" of change may itself force restructuring and policy changes.

SILVER LINING?

Positive results do indeed come from some attempts at postmerger restructuring of companies. As mentioned earlier, today's economy provides opportunities for significant overhaul of company operations and unprofitable units. It is often necessary to create a new identity, so firms will consolidate and integrate systems and procedures. This can result in new structures and subsidiaries to address new markets or opportunities. There is often an aura or a distinct feeling in the moods and morale of employees of a "new wave" or a "breath of fresh air."

Despite initial difficulties, the integration and new corporate identification process (which is inevitable) may indeed go well. But this is often only a silver lining. Much hard work must be done. Corporate culture is significant. Recent experts have repeatedly made the point (Kennedy and Deal, Peters and Waterman, Drucker) that cultures often make the difference between success and failure. Whether or not a corporate culture is supportive and benign makes a huge difference in the quality of life of many individuals.

Chaos shakes up culture. Clashing cultures set up negative processes of conflict, win–lose struggle, and depression. Though the natural cycle of events usually means that the difficulties don't last forever, enormous energies can be spent in the process. Confusion and anxiety, which are natural stages of morale during the early phase of a merger or acquisition, eventually are reduced. Structural changes are made and accepted. Leadership emerges and the survivors become apparent. But what energy! What human potential is involved in the meantime!

If Sony's founder, Morita, is correct, we do have cause for concern. Enormous energies are dissipated, many become victims of takeover trauma, and we become a nation preoccupied with short-term gain. Who is building for the future, let alone minding the store?

If a crisis is pending, then we are looking at the very worst elements that a purely capitalistic society has to offer. Ironically, stockholders are also short-term beneficiaries of the current trends. For them, the crisis is simply a matter of where to invest. Although windfall profits are possible, risk is heightened. Bad investment decisions during major swings in mergers and acquisitions can ruin estates! Indeed this is an arena in which stockholders must become more aware, astute, and perhaps involved.

REDEFINING CORPORATE CULTURE

If there are lessons in all this that would permit a clearer understanding of corporate culture, we need to identify them. It may be that we are seeing a glimpse of an even more important rendering of the corporate culture phenomenon than has been suggested to date.

For example, we know already that corporate culture is manageable and malleable. Managers do in fact change culture, sometimes unwittingly, sometimes by design. And we know that corporate cultures do evolve. Employee behavior conforms to the new set of expectations. Reward systems reinforce the existing culture. If no attention is given to it, old cultural norms may linger. But old culture is out and new culture is "in." And we might actually conclude that culture is not a terribly persistent thing, at least when we are talking about companies. (Countries may be more resilient in their cultural persistence.)

Thus, out of the colliding and clashing of corporate cultures, we discern some interesting new dimensions of corporate culture and social processes. Earlier notions of corporate culture suggest a persistence and frozen nature that we do not see in the cases of culture clash. Indeed, it seems correct to view culture as a temporary and malleable force. Strong executives can manage the process of cultural change to achieve their own ends. Many financially oriented managers totally ignore it, even when they face one of the strongest forms of corporate culture—backlash and overt resistance.

Culture shaping is critical before, during, and after a merger. There is more of an opportunity to take deliberate action than originally thought. It can happen by default, but if managers take charge of the culture-clash and culture-solution processes, smoother transitions are possible. Leaders can be more aware of internal processes and, if given to act in a positive manner, can greatly benefit the change process. But, just as equally, and perhaps just as likely, they can ignore the culture factor and merge companies based only on external factors, such as financial gains, product markets, tax avoidance, and so on.

HARD REALITIES

There is no way that the advanced economic system of our society will prevent complex corporate maneuvering. The rules of the game have gotten more complex. Corporate cultures will clash amid the moves. And there will be an ambience of psychological chaos and confusion. Not everyone can play the game equally well, nor do they all want to.

And some will be winners, some will just survive, and some will lose more than they gain. Thus, in all of this it is important for responsible managers and employees (doesn't that include just about all of us?) to acknowledge the hard realities as well as all the positives. In summary form, these are:

1. Corporate culture clash is unavoidable.
2. This clashing process ultimately gets resolved at some new "equilibrium" in the new corporate culture.

3. The clash has both unproductive and productive consequences. For example, good people are lost, yet they often move on to better career paths.

4. There are more players in the arenas. Investors are more active. External raiders are powerful. Deal-makers can destroy or build vast fortunes overnight.

As the United States aligns itself toward more equality in the trade deficit wars, we may see even more corporate maneuvering in the pursuit of better competitiveness abroad. If a "no more Mr. Nice Guy" attitude prevails, corporate leaders and raiders will become even more tenacious, though mitigated by greater SEC scrutiny of insider dealing. But through the process, long-term thinking may actually emerge. The recent emphasis on quality[9] in American manufacturing and management systems may have diverted attention from what has actually been a more profound shift in the corporations and society—restructuring of macrobusiness units and entities on a grand scale. Merger mania may cool down, and there may be fewer big deals, but a new set of rules of the game may come to the surface:

1. Corporate chaos (restructuring, bankruptcy, leveraged buyouts, mergers, acquisitions, international joint ventures) will become commonplace.

2. Corporate culture clash will become a more managed process. There will be greater social responsibility

attached to orderly transitions of large company entities.

3. Conservative tendencies will provide a countervailing influence. The court system may play a role in "job sovereignty" and job protectionism. Unions will become more astute as players. Raiders may become restrained in their acceptable methods. Insiders will be more carefully checked. In socialist countries, governments may react with restrictions placed upon corporate maneuvering.

As we analyze the future possibilities, it becomes even more difficult when we consider the trends in the larger global picture:

¶   Persistent and perverse trade imbalances between mature, advanced nations

¶   Unprecedented levels of personal and national borrowing

¶   The near-default positions of major country debtors

¶   The rise of protectionism

¶   Unionism on the decline worldwide

Corporate restructuring and reshuffling may have become an economic necessity or, at least, a significant departure from previous business strategies. It provides a new and constructive vista for corporate growth, and one that had not been as fully explored earlier in our history. Its full economic and historical significance is ahead of us, although many of the companies that figure prominently in our childhood memories now have new names or have faded into oblivion.[10]

WHERE HAVE ALL THE PEOPLE GONE?

Back to the silver lining. Not all the news is bad. People do relocate and find better careers after they have been fired or quit. It is true that sometimes it seems as if they disappear; we often cannot locate old friends in lost companies. Companies do go through metamorphoses. Healing takes place.

The energy that comes from a new company spirit can be renewing and invigorating.[11] Managers can have new titles and areas of responsibility. Sometimes the company is a much healthier entity, both financially and psychologically. Often the new leaders are more successful. In theory, this is as it should be. We go on, we learn, we improve, and we grow.

The exciting possibility also exists for the private individual to benefit enormously from surviving and participating in the merger game. Employees increasingly hold stock in the companies where they work. If one were astute enough, one could maneuver investments toward the winning scenario, whether this means holding stock or selling it. The merger-astute employee, regardless of level in the organization, is (theoretically) in a position to be a winner. And though he or she may not have the detailed information possessed by senior management to qualify as an "insider" by SEC terms, the opportunity for seeing the signs of pending change are ever present.

FOR ASTUTE LEADERS

We are interested in the approach taken personally by the top industry leaders in the game of merger mania. It should be said that there are some who play the game totally, it would seem, for what they can get for their own estate. They are driven by greed, wholly bent on ego enhancement and wealth as an end in itself, with no concern for the legal or social costs involved. Fortunately, some of this type of corporate leader (or investment banker) are now identified and are under investigation. Some of those caught have made partial restitution and have even made public apologies. Hardly enough penalty, it would seem, for such flagrant violation of public trust. And there are many who have opportunity for cheating, but who do not. The great majority balance personal wealth as an objective with socially acceptable goals— such as contributing to the company and society. And of these there are a few who can orchestrate their company's destiny and who have the ability to be heavy players of the game, but who still act responsibly. These leaders retain their aggressive stance toward corporate growth and revitalization and are content with their own level of personal wealth. They are still focused on greater good or higher purposes, and they can see deeply within the layers of their corporate cultures. They:

1. Have generally followed a path that has a consideration for corporate history and tradition, though they may know of the need for change.

2. Have identified a path or vision for the corporate direction, including its culture, structure, and people.

3. Verify and remain acutely tuned to culture needs, clashes, and the outcomes of win–lose struggles as they play out in postmerger dramas.

4. Lead people and groups with a personal and non-remote style of leadership through the crisis periods.

5. Commit to *real* net growth and the concept of a full-value company.

THE HIGH-TECH PERSPECTIVE

The experience of counseling many high-tech entrepreneurs and founders of companies has helped us to gain an even clearer perspective with which to view the future. The currently popular stereotype of the high-tech entrepreneur is fairly valid. He or she is an independent type, not a joiner by nature. There is a sense of being "driven" to reach some personal objectives relating to product evolution and acceptance, not necessarily personal financial success. In an interview, an entrepreneur in southern California who has built a $500 million company in seven years remarked: "I have had the pleasure of meeting many successful entrepreneurs, and I have yet to find one that was in it for the money." There is also an ingredient of eccentricity and personal style. Sometimes this is expressed in the individual's management style or as a theme in the company's culture, e.g., all managers are golfers or all managers are heavily involved in personal computers.

The significant common theme is the complete absence of culturally defined structure or "discipline." Things develop out of the personal energy of the entrepreneur. The company makes strides when and only when the founder engineers it. There is an ultimately personal quality to this. It is not progress as others would define and predict it, nor is it necessarily logical. If the entrepreneur has a good sense of innate logic, or trusts a few around him or her who are of the "logical" type, then things may seem to move in predictable directions. But in the majority of cases, they do not. They move when and where the leader moves. And most of the time that is in creative and successful directions.

This style of management is in stark contrast to the value systems espoused in most training programs and in our best business schools. It is also quite different from the movement in the late sixties and seventies called "organizational development" (OD), in which consultants worked with senior managers and leaders to bring about "planned change" or, as Gordon Lippitt has put it, "organizational renewal." These programs presume a rational process, rational players, and rational states of mind. In most organizational development training, for example, crisis management is to be discouraged. Information sharing and decision-making, on the other hand, are to be broadened and expanded toward participatory modes of managing.

For some "true" entrepreneurs, this is anathema! The preferred style is one of responding to the "now," whether placid or in crisis mode, moving toward the unknown, and striving for maximum stimulation. The entrepreneur-founder has no time for distractions, and his or her loyal executives typically have been acculturated to this style, desirable or not.

Thus, in the United States today we have mixed models of corporate leadership. Some are traditional and straight out of the management textbooks; others defy neat description. And these styles are moving corporations and fueling economic growth. Through this mix, and perhaps because of it, we are presented with a model of the revitalized American corporation, which is more dynamic than ever before. Though its dynamism is still evolving, we have a mosaic that we can describe and that may suggest the destiny of the merger–acquisition trend. It includes:

1. Opportunism—the real drive to excel in world and domestic markets, achieve "real value" for stockholders, and maximize gain for founders.

2. Conservatism coupled with the personal style of founders-owners. The trend is to get lean internally, yet retain personality and spirit.

3. Cultural yet not culture-bound. Corporate culture is inevitable. Corporations should manage their cultures, not vice versa.

4. Some corporate builders and leaders do appear to be capable of managing toward some notion of higher good or greater welfare, not just for their own purposes or estates.

5. Some leaders appear to be building empires and playing the "casino economy" for its maximum yield. This will add to what some have called the "sleaze factor" in the modern economy.

CORPORATE DESTINIES

Companies come from somewhere and are going somewhere. But they do not exist forever. To the point, they are changing and adapting at an increasingly faster rate. Some organizations are sacred, it would seem, and are likely to be here as long as one can imagine (such as General Motors, Hilton Hotels, IBM, General Electric, etc.). Yet even this is unclear. Who in the sixties might have thought that we would not have RCA or Gulf Oil with us today? Companies merge, acquire, go bankrupt, change name and form with almost no regard for tradition! What can we expect for our future corporate America?

Life after merger mania can be good, indeed! We have seen that many of the changes are necessary. The changes bring hope to a cynical world:

¶ There may just be a revitalization of corporate structure amid the chaos.

¶ The workforce is becoming more astute about how to invest in winners and how to defend against merger mania gone wild.[12]

¶ Leaders have more people watching them as they attempt to navigate toward *real, net growth*, not growth by the "sleaze" factor of the "casino effect."

¶ Stockholders are becoming more tuned to corporate strategies for growth and are listening to the raiders who may even be good news for the corporate future.

CAN EVERYONE WIN?

Culture clashing is inevitable when dissimilar corporations are merged. But the noise of the clash may be music to the ears of stockholders who have long awaited change. Coalitions will be in conflict. Employees, unions, stockholders, and customers all represent differing interests.

But there are self-correcting mechanisms. And some of the conflict is very healthy, though individuals may lose money or jobs in the process. That all interests, at every moment of the cycle, would be equally satisfied is unrealistic. It is also not what the system stands for. Corporate chaos, for some, may be the stuff of fortunes and winning destinies. For others, their companies will not make it, and the losses may seem exaggerated. But we are all learning, or should be at least, through the cycles of merging and cultural blending that our best managers are grappling with in their daily routine. Living with and learning from this chaotic strain, though only part of the music, is the only choice we have. It will make some of us stronger and even better at winning. Out of the debris of merger mania in the years to come, corporate America will produce some world-class champions. Winners at home, winners in professional arenas, and winners for a longer game.

EXECUTIVE SUMMARY

- Mergers and acquisitions have both positive and negative impacts.

- Corporate culture can be reshaped in the aftermath of a merger or acquisition. This process is slow and difficult, but the payoff is enormous.

- American trends of corporate restructuring are part of a global pattern.

- There is a method to the madness. Corporate traditions and cultures create inertia. This momentum makes it possible to predict patterns of behavior, i.e., corporate destinies.

ENDNOTES

1. An excellent recent book on the technical side is Joseph Marren's *Mergers and Acquisitions: Will You Overpay?* (Homewood, Ill.: Dow Jones-Irwin, 1985).
2. Lawrence, John, "Merger Mania: House of Cards May Collapse," *Los Angeles Times*, 15 February 1987, IV.
3. See Drucker, Peter, *Innovation and Entrepreneurship: Practice and Principles* (New York: Harper and Row, 1985).
4. See discussion in *Business Week*, "What the Rally Really Means," 2 February 1987, pp. 58–62. Also, the excellent book by John Naisbitt and Patricia Aburdene, *Re-inventing the Corporation* (New York: Warner Books, 1985).
5. Morita, Akio, and the Sony Corporation, *Made in Japan* (New York: Dutton, 1986).
6. Law, Warren, "A Corporation Is More Than Its Stock," *Harvard Business Review*, May–June 1986, p. 80.
7. "Pickens Defends Takeovers," *San Diego Tribune*, 4 December 1986, p. AA-1.
8. "Santa Fe Southern Hopes to Get Back on Track," *Los Angeles Times*, 9 November 1986, IV.
9. See Albrecht, Karl and Zemke, Ron, *Service America: Doing Business in the New Economy* (Homewood, Ill.: Dow Jones–Irwin, 1985); Crosby, Philip, *Quality Is Free* (New York: Mentor Books, 1979).
10. Groves, Martha, " '86 Merger Mania Changed the Face of State's Retailers," *Los Angeles Times*, 11 January 1987, IV; "NBC, Group W May Merge Radio Outlets," *San Diego Tribune*, 17 October 1986, p. AA-1.

11. See Miller, Larry, *American Spirit: Visions of a New Corporate Culture* (New York: Morrow and Co., 1984).
12. One of the more interesting examples is that of "silver parachutes"—all full-time employees get at least one year's salary if they are fired after a hostile takeover (for other than just cause). See *Forbes*, 3 November 1986, p. 8.

10

WHERE DO WE GO FROM HERE?

What have we learned from all this? First, let us say that this book attempts to position the state of affairs and current thinking, not to offer definitive solutions. There are identifiable stakeholders—each with their own perceived threats and opportunities. This book has held the reader at each of those places for a moment to see the whole. Even the interactions of the various key segments are not always rational or reciprocal. Most of the time, it is a nonlogical, political game. Some are winning, some are losing.

CHAOS OR CONVERGENCE?

In the chaos of the moment, we see signs of the past. In each industrial era we see signs of the management styles needed for the next. In today's postindustrial period, we see the need for managing with more flexible styles and skills. Some have called this transformational management. The onus is clearly on the executive and leader to facilitate the changeover *at the same time* as managing in the usual, proactive way. Some will be called on to manage very large scale corporate organizations—mega-systems in the new age of meta-industrial change. Their job will be to manage through the cycles of merger and acquisition, to shape entirely new corporations, and to reshape the character of the corporation. How is this possible?

THE BRUTAL FACT OF LIFE

Life is change. The pace is accelerating, and some trauma is inevitable. Coping skills are a must. Organizational change and transformation skills are critical for the new-age manager. It is not enough to be able to handle problems when they arise—managers must be able to anticipate the challenges and become proactive or "preventative."[1] One's view must adopt change as a "friend"—it will be ongoing. Perhaps the highest state of the managing art will be that area in which one will have the opportunity to promote "new life" amid the chaos and trauma—synergy between the differing entities.[2]

CORPORATE SYNERGY

A few managers will be able to:

¶ Help others to survive and understand (possibly even appreciate) the change process.

¶ Survive actual job shakeup and radical change while remaking the job into something new and better than before.

¶ Help others in human ways, giving new life, trust, friendship, teamwork, and love to others who badly need help (for some will not care).

¶ Reshape new ideas, norms, codes of work into new corporate character.

¶ Inspire others with their hope for the future.

HEALTHY TRAUMA

This era will test our best and brightest. It will also test our collective management wisdom and intelligence. In American business and academia reside the most advanced state of organization theory and management know-how. The next decades of corporate chaos, restructuring, and change will test that acumen, and we will find out if it is truly a valuable national resource or a cultural artifact in time warp. Much of the verdict will be determined not by the millions of employees and managers caught in corporate chaos, but by the deal-makers and power brokers who are shaping corporate destinies.

THE ROLE OF GOVERNMENT

In recent years, state and federal courts have upheld state regulation of takeover activity. Already some of the great

corporate entities have benefited from protective legislation and court rulings. A brief sample:

State:	Protected:
Arizona	Greyhound Bus Lines
Minnesota	Dayton-Hudson
Washington	Boeing
Massachusetts	Gillette
Florida	Harcourt Brace Jovanovich
North Carolina	Burlington Industries

Some of this protection has come at the urging of
threatened managements, something that has led T.
Boone Pickens, Jr., to conduct a national campaign to
raise public awareness as to the possibility of blame
shifting by senior management. Pickens argues that
entrenched managements attempt to cover up their
inefficacy by lobbying against the raiders and explaining
away the "undervaluation of their securities."[3] But the
interesting logic of such campaigns is pitted against the
rising tide of popular support for protective legislation.
Unions, community groups impacted by restructuring,
and some management spokesmen have been the loudest
to respond thus far. And the legislatures and courts have
sensed their ultimate political strength! By September
1987, 26 states had joined the antimerger bandwagon,
with more to follow. A political action group has formed
with the austere name "Coalition to Stop the Raid on

America" with the special focus of protecting small towns caught in merger battles.

MERGER AND ACQUISITION: INTERNATIONAL TRENDS

The global deal-maker's time is yet to come. But the global movements of ownership have certainly begun. And there is evidence to suggest that other countries' deal-makers are learning about the advanced techniques of their seasoned US counterparts. Hostile takeovers are a relatively new phenomenon in Japan, yet they are on the rise. Japanese merger and acquisition activity overall has lagged behind that in the United States, but the gap is closing. One Japanese expert recently summarized the inevitable:

> Every company is now reviewing the situation. The time will come when companies can no longer afford a sense of shame if they want to survive. It will happen within three years.[4]

Courts and state legislation may serve to limit merger and acquisition impact in hometown America but can hardly stop foreign owners and corporate giants from buying small pieces of US companies. In fact, global corporate shakeout has already begun in many specialized industries that rely on international markets and trade. The chance that US industries would in fact enjoy real protection from this larger pattern is remote in the longer term, regardless of individual states' efforts to secure corporate continuities at home. In some cases, if international linkage is not permitted, total bankruptcy could become the only business alternative.

ENDNOTES

1. Harris, Philip R., "Synergistic Strategies for Organization Development," *Leadership and Organizational Development Journal*, Vol. 2, No. 3, 1981, pp. 27–32.
2. Harris, Philip, R. and Moran, Robert T., *Managing Cultural Synergy* (Houston: Gulf Publishing, 1982). See Chapters 1, 6, 15.
3. Pickens, T. Boone, Jr., "Professions of a Short Timer," *Harvard Business Review*, May–June 1986, pp. 75–79.
4. Yamamoto, Takayuki, "M&A Japanese Style," *Business Tokyo*, September 1987, p. 9.

APPENDICES

APPENDIX A: INTROSPECTIVE SURVEY FOR MANAGERS FACING CORPORATE CHAOS

Collect data and reach a conclusion on each item:

1. Current owners and leaders?
2. History of company?
3. Outside challengers and motives?
4. Changes in competitors?
5. List several possible scenarios?

. . . at first sign of change . . .

6. What scenario is starting?
7. Who is leading?
8. Motives of various players?
9. Best case for you?
10. Worst case for you?
11. Who really knows . . . can you find out?

. . . getting specific about your stake . . .

12. Do you own stock?
13. Value now . . . value later?
14. Retirement package intact or damaged?
15. Will you get "parachute" . . . value?
16. Better to exit and go to competitor now?
17. Career change?

. . . positioning for winning . . .

18. What is your larger stake?
19. New job . . . promotion . . . title?
20. New stock options . . . benefits?
21. Invest your extra money now?
22. New skills needed?
23. New boss, mentor, champion needed?
24. New personal attitude toward future?

Musts:

Evaluate all of above
Reality test your answers in confidence
Leave a loser or become a player and a winner!

APPENDIX B: CORPORATE LEADER'S "CONSCIENCE" CHECKLIST

1. What was the original source of the merger–acquisition idea? Who? When?

2. If yours, when did you first conceive of it? Why? How might it relate to your own career plan or ambition?

3. Who are the other beneficiaries?

4. Who gets hurt? How? How do you rationalize this impact?

5. What is your vision of the merger scenario?

6. How do the business units complement each other?

7. How do the cultures of the companies get impacted?

8. What are the immediate losses? What gets lost in the process?

9. What is your specific strategy for making the post-merger transition? For the cultural blending?

10. What resources or helpful mechanisms are in place to use in the transition of corporate cultures?

11. What will the new corporate structure look like?

12. Who are the new leaders? What plans for identifying them?

APPENDIX C: HOW YOU CAN TELL IF YOUR FIRM IS APPROACHING CHAOS

Your firm is about to take over another in the same or related industry. . . .

... there are competitors that are poorly managed, and their stock is undervalued!

... there are conspicuous and sudden changes in products or services that are out of context or seem strange!

... high-level executives are seen with those from competing companies—beware of friendly relations!

... senior executives are absent or low profile for regular and frequent periods!

... your company has experienced rapid and healthy growth in new product or high-tech areas.

... you hear rumors ... ask questions ... and don't get answers! There seems to be hedging or dodging of direct inquiries. There may even be outright denials.

... the founder has no heirs!

... the founder and senior group are all older individuals and have not seemed to be active in developing any prominent successors.

APPENDIX D: WHEN TAKEOVER MAY BE NEAR—WHAT TO LOOK FOR IN YOUR COMPANY

Ownership Factor:
Founders and owners are old and approaching retirement.

There are no sons or daughters, or they are in other businesses.

Owner dies suddenly, and spouse is not involved in the business.

Stock Value:
Stock is severely undervalued or overvalued.

Stock is all privately held, and rumors say the company should or could go public.

There is high value in proprietary products for competitors.

The company has enjoyed unique markets, one-of-a-kind markets, or has a competitive edge.

Management Structure:
There are rumors of mass firings, layoffs, or "bad management."

Managers leave and set up their own companies.

There appears to be "fat" or redundancy in the organizational staffing structure.

Managers are disgruntled and speak openly about either exceedingly positive or negative company policies.

Physical Signs:
The company appears to hold onto valuable real estate assets that have no direct connection to operations.

There are swarms of out-of-town professionals with briefcases who visit the most senior executives.

Envelopes are marked "CONFIDENTIAL" with guarded secrecy.

New security guards appear overnight.

Physical assets are sold off suddenly with little or no explanation (airplanes, trucks, buildings, equipment, etc.).

Presidents are increasingly absent and hold secret meetings out of town.

Product or Market Signs:
Competitors seem to match up with extreme "fit" or complementary product lines.

Competitors' geographical territories work toward some new or overall pattern; there is fit or congruence.

Wall Street, brokerage, or financial analysts are seen or heard to be looking at the product or conducting "market analyses."

Any of these signs may or *may not* indicate some underlying movement or takeover maneuvering. Several of these taken together might indicate a greater likelihood that something is afoot. Then, also, there are other signs not listed here that might be highly indicative of activity. Interestingly, most people, as shoppers, consumers, and even as employees, do not make it their habit to study and notice the isolated pieces of the flow of events that could be the secret key to destiny scenarios! If we only made it our business, might we not be more astute in our world?

Contemplate your next trip to the nearby mall or to the city to shop. Might you just be looking at some winners? And, of course, some places where you should not spend your time and money?

APPENDIX E: VISIONING EXERCISE FOR LEADERS OF CORPORATE CULTURE

1. Identify your parents' and grandparents' wishes for you and your success. Why? What was their life script and scenario?

2. Identify your earliest childhood vision of your career. Then your next one, and so on, through early adulthood. What were the main themes?

3. What kind of company and company leader were you exposed to early in your life?

4. What kind did you dislike? What kind, if any, did you abhor?

5. Did you ever make any self-promises ("If I ever run a company, I will make sure to . . . .")?

6. Are you now a company leader? Do you have check-writing privileges? Do you have destiny-writing privileges?

7. Does your philosophy allow you to define and design your ideal company scenario of success?

8. Do you want to do this at this time in your career? In the company's career?

9. Should others participate? Who? How much?

10. Design something in your mind.*

11. Allow time for thought and discussion with trusted others to reshape and clarify the form and the feelings that accompany the idea. Reality test with objective others you can trust.

12. Set about it!

---

*There is no one best or precise way to visualize an ideal corporate structure or company scenario in your mind. Most people who have tried and enjoyed this exercise have done this while relaxed, with a good pen and tablet, alone in one of their favorite settings. They think about best cases and worst ones. They think about how they want to be treated. And about how they want to shape their team and employees' attitudes toward the industry, toward the community, and toward each other. Some think of religion and frankly see their company as an externalization of their belief system and their faith or lack of it in the future, and in fellow others. Some think of death and how they want it to be if they're suddenly taken from the scene. Others plan out the retirement and the specifics of divesting, and the impact on others.

This all takes time and emotion. There will be an ideational (form) and an emotional side to the vision of a future company culture, based on the most personal and subjective parts of the leader, as well as the most practical, "worldly" side. Even if a vision is never consciously held (a statement that we challenge), a corporate culture is, by default, from the leader's subjective reality, a choicepoint. If no discussion or introspection is ever done, some corporate destiny will unfold that will be the responsibility and the burden of the leader to bear. Some of these leaders in our experience seem to be very conscious about it all, do much soul-searching for their own role, and soul-searching for the corpus of the business as well.

APPENDIX F: WRITING YOUR DESTINY SCENARIO (FOR CORPORATE LEADERS)

The Five Basic Choices in life:

1. Grow your company and acquire others. Build an empire!

2. Build it up and sell it off. Retire and enjoy your success.

3. Struggle along until it's time to retire. Try to sell it for what it's worth, or give it away.

4. Get out before it is time to really commit yourself and your whole life. Stay afoot, change careers. Become a follower.

5. Work for others. Always wonder "what if . . . ."

Now, ask yourself these questions with respect to the above choices:

¶ What did my father/mother do?

¶ Who are my teachers, mentors, role models? What did they do?

¶ Which choice is most rewarding?

¶ Which is most degrading?

¶ Which one says the most about what I stand for?

¶ Which one gives me the longest life?

¶ Which gives me the shortest life?

¶ What are the tradeoffs between the most attractive choices?

¶ Where is my company now?

¶ What themes does my company have going now?

¶ What themes need close examination, perhaps changing?

¶ What is the specific winning scenario?

¶ Who will champion it? If not I, who? Can I find someone who wants to do it for him/herself and me?

¶ If we cannot define a winning course, why not?

¶ If we cannot define one, what are the specific obstacles, and can they be challenged?

¶ If it is not obstacles, is it my energy level? Do I really want to do anything special?

¶ If it is OK to be unambitious, or to work for others, when and where did I make that decision?

¶ What would it take for me to look again at that?

¶ Will I really be happy with the theme of what happens to my company?

¶ Are its destiny and mine the same?

GLOSSARY

Acquisition premium   An acquisition premium is the amount paid for an acquisition in excess of the preacquisition stock price. These can be 40–50% and more, thus making acquisitions very expensive. Large acquisition premia are one reason why acquisitions have performed poorly for many corporations.

Antitakeover devices   These are techniques used by corporations to make it difficult or impossible for an outsider (such as a raider) to acquire the firm. Antitakeover devices may include voting provisions for the board, selling off prized assets, or a variety of other financial maneuvers.

Asset stripping   This is an acquisition strategy used by some raiders for personal gain. Asset stripping involves the purchase of a firm and immediate sale of many or all of its assets, thus resulting in the loss of jobs for many employees. Asset stripping is based on the belief that a mismanaged firm is worth more when liquidated in pieces than as a combined operating entity (the whole is worth less than the sum of the parts).

Conglomerates   These are large firms composed of many unrelated businesses. The largest conglomerates (Litton, Gulf + Western, ITT) were built from hundreds of acquisitions.

Core   Those most key, most essential (perhaps few) elements of a corporate culture that are the subset from which the organization derives its character, culture, and climate.

Corporate character   The particular uniqueness of a corporate organization. This includes the corporate values and ethical system.

Corporate climate   The psychological mood, or mind-set, within a company. Also known as "morale."

Corporate culture   Normally defined to include values, norms, rites, roles, ceremonies within organizations. The culture is the aggregate. It has structure and dynamic qualities, since culture is essentially always "in process."

Destiny   The notion of a company's future. It will have one, even if it is a bankruptcy scenario. That future will exist at any moment as a state of conditions and a configuration of things, people, processes. There will be a particular path to that future state, and a "string" of future states constitutes that path to destiny.

Divestiture   The flip side of acquisitions: Divestitures involve the sale of portions of a firm to another company. Divestitures can lead to a reorganization of the division and the loss of jobs.

Escalating momentum   A form of self-fulfilling prophecy. The reality of takeover is fueled by an increasing factor of expected outcomes and resulting emotional swings. This process can include rapid changes in morale, anxiety, rumors, and somatic illnesses of employees.

Friendly takeover   This is an acquisition where the target firm does not object to being purchased. An example of a friendly takeover is when a **white knight** rescues a firm from a **hostile takeover**.

Greenmail   This is a form of bribe paid to potential takeover threats (often raiders) to prevent the acquisition. Greenmail can entail hundreds of millions of dollars in payments in order to protect the interests of entrenched management.

Hostile takeover   This is an acquisition in which the target firm is opposed to the purchase. In a hostile takeover (see **raiders**), the target firm may adopt some form of **antitakeover device** or seek the aid of a **white knight**.

Iceberg model   A conventional conceptual model for analyzing and understanding organizations and their core, character, culture, climate, details, etc.

Inside information   Usually refers to very privileged financial or strategic information that only very top board members or executives have. The power of this information is that large gains can be realized by playing stock purchases or sales based on anticipated swings in market price. Insiders have, if they transact based on their insider knowledge, a distinct and "unfair" advantage over public investors.

Investment banking This is the industry of brokering financial transactions for corporations, including mergers and acquisitions. Investment banking is the glamour career of the eighties, in which young MBAs have found the fast track to millions.

Junk bonds Junk bonds are a form of acquisition financing often used in leveraged buyouts. These are bonds with a very low rating and may place the corporation in jeopardy of future default.

Leveraged buyout This is a form of acquisition in which very little equity capital is used by the firm (or managers) making the acquisition. The acquisition is primarily financed through the use of debt, often creating such extreme leverage that the bonds take on a very low rating (see **junk bonds**). In a leveraged buyout, it is nearly possible to acquire a firm with its own assets as capital.

MBA fever The popular belief that an MBA degree from a prestigious graduate school is the requisite "ticket to admission" to the corporate world of action, including merger, takeover drama, and investing or gambling with investments.

Merger mania A phrase used by insider Ivan Boesky to refer to the flurry of takeovers, mergers, acquisitions, and major corporate transformations. It refers to both the activity pattern and the aggregate psychological state of mind produced by such activity.

Poison pill A poison pill is a form of antitakeover device that makes the target firm less attractive as an acquisition candidate. Poison pills may include the liquidation of valuable assets or the passing of provisions that create financial penalties for any firm which attempts an acquisition. Poison pills are usually employed to protect the interest of an entrenched management team.

Psychological warfare A chaotic state of morale that results when an acquiring company plots to demoralize the takeover target. Tactics include rumors, threatened layoffs, phasing out products, name changes, and leadership changes.

Postmerger integration A process of consolidating corporate culture and corporate practices after a merger takes place. A complex process that is unique to each case.

Raiders These are individuals who earn fortunes by making hostile takeovers of companies. They seek corporations that have low stock prices and may even use the assets of the target firm as collateral to finance the purchase. Raiders have developed reputations as ruthless businessmen who let nothing stand in the way of their personal wealth.

Restructuring This is an umbrella term applied to the various forms of corporate reorganizations that have become popular during the last ten years (such as acquisitions and divestitures). Restructuring is a means for firms to abandon traditional lines of business and to enter new and more promising industries.

Scorched earth   A form of antitakeover device in which the target firm makes itself unattractive by purposely ruining a valuable part of its business. This is similar to **selling the crown jewels**.

Selling the crown jewels   An antitakeover device in which the target firm divests itself of its most valuable assets—which were probably the real target of the threatened hostile takeover. See **scorched earth**.

Steward   A person who theoretically represents a fair-minded, objective, and supportive stance or role in a corporation. Outside directors, appointed for their wisdom and knowledge, are stewards. The corporate "good" is put in their hands.

Synergy   The elusive notion that two firms will be worth more operating as a team than as independent entities. Synergy is the driving logic behind many acquisitions.

Vision   That mental picture of a corporation's future state which is held at any moment in the mind of a person. It can have huge dimensions and detail and can be a great source of motivation and desire. Entrepreneurs and "eagles" typically have vision.

White knight   A firm that comes to the rescue of the target of a hostile takeover. A white knight will usually acquire the same firm under more attractive provisions, such as a guarantee of the retention of management and other employees.

REFERENCES

Baker, E.L. "Managing Organizational Culture." *Management Review*, July 1980, pp. 8–13.

Bianco, A., Schiller, Z., Therrien, L., and Rothman, M. "A Flurry of Greenmail Has Stockholders Cursing." *Business Week*, 8 December 1986, pp. 32–34.

"Carl Icahn: Raider or Manager?" *Business Week*, 27 October 1986, pp. 98–104.

"Deal Mania." *Business Week*, 24 November 1986, pp. 74–93.

Dobrzynski, J.H. "Splitting Up." *Business Week*, 1 July 1985, pp. 50–55.

Dodd, P. "Merger Proposals, Management Discretion and Stockholder Wealth." *Journal of Financial Economics*, June 1980, pp. 113–138.

Drucker, P. *People and Performance: The Best of Peter Drucker on Management*. New York: Harper & Row, 1977.

Dwyer, P., Glaberson, W.P., and Norman, J.P. "Delaware's Grand Masters of the Merger Game." *Business Week*, pp. 90–92.

Ehrlich, E. "Twilight for the Lone Raider?" *Business Week*, 27 January 1986, pp. 38–39.

Elgers, P.T. and Clark, J.J. "Merger Types and Shareholder Returns: Additional Evidence." *Financial Management*, Summer 1980, pp. 66–72.

Farrell, C. "Investors Can Still Profit from the Merger Game." *Business Week*, 24 November 1986, p. 96.

Fisher, A.B. "Oops! My Company Is on the Block." *Fortune*, 23 July 1984, pp. 16–21.

"Frank Lorenzo, High Flier." *Business Week*, 10 March 1986, pp. 104–107.

Glaberson, W.B., Rothman, M., and Ivey, M. "Chapter 11 Isn't So Chic Anymore." *Business Week*, 16 June 1986, p. 35.

Greenwald, J. "The Popular Game of Going Private." *Time*, 4 November 1985, pp. 54–55.

Harris, P. R. "Synergistic Strategies for Organization Development." *Leadership and Organization Development Journal*, Vol. 2, No. 3, 1981, pp. 27–32.

Harris, P. R. and Moran, R. T. *Managing Cultural Differences*. Houston: Gulf Publishing, 1979.

Hector, G. "Are Shareholders Cheated by LBOs?" *Fortune*, 19 January 1987, pp. 98–104.

Hofer, C.W. and Schendel, D. *Strategy Formulation: Analytical Concepts*. St. Paul: West Publishing Co., 1978.

Houston, P. and Hawkins, C. "Republic Will Help Northwest Put the Heat on United." *Business Week*, 10 February 1986, p. 27.

"Irv the Liquidator Tries to Live Down His Name." *Business Week*, 19 March 1984, pp. 70–71.

Jemison, D. and Sitkin, S. B. "Corporate Acquisitions: A Process Perspective." *Academy of Management Review*, 1, 1986, pp. 145–163.

Jensen, M.C. "Takeovers: Folklore and Science." *Harvard Business Review*, November–December 1984, pp. 109–121.

Keller, J.J. "A Leaner AT&T Could Cost Thousands of Jobs." *Business Week*, 15 September 1986, p. 80.

Kitching, J. "Why Do Mergers Miscarry?" *Harvard Business Review*, November–December 1967.

Leighton, C.M. and Tod, G.R. "After the Acquisition: Continuing Challenge." *Harvard Business Review*, March–April 1969.

"Leveraged Buyouts: How Real Are the Dangers?" *Business Week*, 2 July 1984, pp. 72–74.

Levine, J.B., Melcher, R.A., Carson, T., and Bartlett, S. "Wells Fargo May Have Bagged a Bargain in Crocker." *Business Week*, 24 February 1986, p. 35.

Lowenstein, L. "No More Cozy Management Buyouts." *Harvard Business Review*, January–February 1986, pp. 147–156.

MacMillan, I.C. and Jones, P.E. *Strategy Formulation: Power and Politics,* 2d ed. St. Paul: West Publishing Co., 1978.

Madrick, J. *Taking America: How We Got from the First Hostile Takeover to Megamergers, Corporate Raiding and Scandal.* Bantam Books, 1987.

Magnet, M. "Acquiring without Smothering." *Fortune*, 12 November 1984, pp. 22–30.

Magnet, M. "Help! My Company Has Just Been Taken Over." *Fortune*, 9 July 1984, pp. 44–51.

Magnet, M. "What Merger Mania Did to Syracuse." *Fortune*, 3 February 1986, pp. 94–98.

Mandelker, G. "Risk and Return: The Case of Merging Firms." *Journal of Financial Economics*, December 1974, pp. 303–335.

Marks, M. "The Human Side of Corporate Merger." *Los Angeles Times*, 30 August 1987, p. IV, 3.

Mason, T. and Wallace, G.D. "The Downfall of a CEO." *Business Week*, 16 February 1987, pp. 76–84.

McComas, M. "After the Buyout, Life Isn't Easy." *Fortune*, 9 December 1985, pp. 42–47.

Mirvis, P. and Marks, M.L. "Merger Syndrome: Stress and Uncertainty." *Mergers and Acquisitions*, Summer 1985, pp. 50–55.

Mirvis, P. and Marks, M.L. "Merger Syndrome: Management by Crisis." *Mergers and Acquisitions*, January/ February 1986, pp. 70–76.

Mueller, D.C. "The Effects of Conglomerate Mergers: A Survey of the Empirical Evidence." *Journal of Banking and Finance*, 1, 1977, pp. 315–347.

Naisbitt, J. and Aburdene, P. *Reinventing the Corporation*. New York: Warner Books, Inc., 1985.

Nielsen, J. "The Raider Who Kept TWA Flying." *Fortune*, 5 January 1987, p. 63.

Norton, R.E. "Tinkering around with Corporate Takeovers." *Fortune*, 3 February 1986, p. 101.

Peters, J.P. and Waterman, R.H., Jr. *In Search of Excellence: Lessons from America's Best-Run Companies*. New York: Harper & Row, 1982.

Petre, P. "Merger Fees That Bend the Mind." *Fortune*, 20 January 1986, pp. 18–23.

Pettigrew, A.M. "On Studying Organizational Cultures." *Administrative Science Quarterly*, December 1979, pp. 570–581.

Pickens, T. B. "Professions of a Short-Termer." *Harvard Business Review*, May–June 1986, pp. 75–79.

Porter, M. *Competitive Strategy*. New York: The Free Press, 1980.

Prokesch, S.E. and Powell, W.J. "Do Mergers Really Work?" *Business Week*, 3 June 1985, pp. 88–91.

Rosenfeld, J.D. "Additional Evidence on the Relation between Divestiture Announcements and Shareholder Wealth." *The Journal of Finance*, December 1984, pp. 1437–1448.

Rumelt, R.P. *Strategy, Structure and Economic Performance*. Boston: Division of Research, Graduate School of Business Administration, Harvard University, 1974.

Sales, A.L. and Mirvis, P.H. "When Cultures Collide: Issues in Acquisition." In Kimberly, J.R. and Quinn, R.E. (Eds.). *Managing Organization Transitions*. Homewood, Ill: Irwin, pp. 107–133.

Salter, M.S. and Weinhold, W.A. *Diversification through Acquisition: Strategies for Creating Economic Value*. New York: Macmillan, 1979.

Scherschel, P.M. "The Empire Builders Take Over." *U.S. News & World Report*, 24 November 1986, pp. 49–50.

Schiller, Z. and Rossant, J. "Deals, Deals, Deals: Mergers, Buyouts, Takeovers—the Pace Is Faster Than Ever." *Business Week*, 17 November 1986, pp. 64–65.

Schwartz, H. and Davis, S.M. "Matching Corporate Culture and Business Strategy." *Organizational Dynamics*, Summer 1981, pp. 30–48.

Schwieger, D. and Ivancevich, J. "Executive Actions for Managing Human Resources before and after Acquisition." *Academy of Management Executive*, Vol. 1, No. 2, 1987, pp. 127–138.

Shrivastava, P. "Postmerger Integration." *The Journal of Business Strategy*, Vol. 5, No. 3, pp. 103–111.

Tracy, E.J. "Parachutes A-Popping." *Fortune*, 31 March 1986, p. 66.

Trice, H.M. and Beyer, J.M. "Studying Organizational Cultures through Rites and Ceremonials." *Academy of Management Review*, 1984, pp. 653–669.

"Why Leveraged Buyouts Are Getting So Hot." *Business Week*, 27 June 1983, p. 86.

"Why Rebuilding RCA Is Taking So Much Time." *Business Week*, 7 March 1983, pp. 35–36.

INDEX

acquisitions, 85, 225
airlines, 124–126
antitakeover device, 225
arbitrageur, 65
"asset stripping," 225

bankers, 64, 102, 228
bankruptcy, creative,
   123–125
Behr, Peter, 41
Bendix, 91
Bernard, Chester, 13
Beyer, Jan, 44
board, corporate, 142, 149
Boesky, Ivan, 99
brokers, 64, 102

"Casino Economy," 64, 202
chaos, 1, 138, 148, 153, 190,
   194, 207, 216
Chapter 11, 123
character, corporate, 12, 226
Chiarella and Dirks, 69
climate, corporate, 10, 139,
   226

conglomerate strategies, 112,
   226
Continental Airlines,
   124–125, 135
consultants, 131, 143
core, iceberg, 14, 17–25, 226
culture, corporate, 11,
   141–142, 191–193, 226
culture clash, 47, 194
"culture club," 43, 48, 51
culture shaping, 192

Dart & Kraft, 142
Davis, Stanley, 44
deals, 86–88
DeNoble, Alex, 44
destiny, corporate, 3, 179,
   201–202, 222–223, 226
diversification, 114
divestiture, 114–117, 120,
   226

Eagle school, 40, 51
emotion, 162–163
empire building, 83

entrepreneur, 41, 198–199
escalating momentum, 227
espionage, corporate, 149
"excellence," corporate, vii,
 113

Fallows, James, 64, 186
father-son relationship, 61
followership, 130, 133–135
full value economy, 187
Fuqua Industries, 118
futures, corporate, 49

General Electric, 118
General Motors, 72
Goethe, 16
government, 209–211
greenmail, 227
growth, corporate, 113
Gulf + Western, 121–123

Hallorin, Keith, 44
Harris, Thomas, 130
healing, 171
Heublein, 1
high tech, 198
honeymoon stage, 150
hysteria, corporate, 168

Iacocca, Lee, 92
Icahn, Carl, 72, 93–98
iceberg, corporate, 14, 153,
 168, 227

image, corporate, 25
insider, 66, 188, 227
institutional fiction, 166
intelligence stage, 149
integration, 130
international trends, 211

Jacobs, Irwin, 123
Jamison & Sitkin, 46
"jungle" management theory,
 52
junk bonds, 228

Kitching, John, 44
Koontz, Howard, 52

leadership, 130, 197, 215
leadership fiction, 167
legislation, 50, 209–211
leveraged buyout (LBO),
 103, 228
Lorenzo, Frank, 125
LTV Corp, 68

MacMillan, Ian, 42
Martin Marietta, 91
mavericks, 61
"MBA fever," 228
McKinsey & Co., 89, 111
"merger mania," 88, 228
mergers, 85
Mervis, Philip, 44, 46
Miller, James B., 50

Mitton, Daryl, 42
morale, 139-141
Morita, 187, 191

Naisbitt, John, 179

opportunism, 200
optimism, 170
organizational renewal, 200
organization development,
   176–179, 199

perception, 164–166
personality (corporate), 13
pessimism, 186–188
Peters, Tom, 113
placebo, 177
planning phase, 145
planners, 39
poison pill, 229
Porter, Michael, 42
postmerger integration, 45,
   229
Potts, Mark, 41
powerlessness, 164
psychological warfare, 147,
   229
public courtship, 149

raiders, 60, 76, 93, 229
redundancy, 136

research, 39
resistance, 146
restructuring, 119, 189, 195,
   229
Reynolds, 1
Rumelt, Richard, 114
rumors, 99

Sales, Amy, 44
Schein, Ed, 140
Schwartz, Howard, 44
"scorched earth," 230
script, 63, 130
"selling the crown jewels,"
   230
Sony, 187, 191
stewards, 78, 230
stockholders, 71, 90
strategic complexity, 118
stress, 170
structural consideration, 130
structure, organization,
   136–138
survivor mentality, 172
synergy, 39, 230
synthesis, 50
systems approach, 151

takeover, 99, 217–220, 227
"thingified abstractions," 165
trauma, 209
triage, vii, 173–176

Trice, Harry, 44
Tunstall, W. Brooks, 44

union busting, 59, 73–76
unions, 72

UNISYS, 141, 177
USX, 72

vision, leadership, 220, 230

Williams, Lawrence K., vii

Here's how to receive your free catalog and save money on your next book order from Scott, Foresman and Company:

Simply mail in the response card below to receive your free copy of our latest catalog featuring business and computer books. After you've looked through the catalog and you're ready to place your order, attach the coupon below to receive $1.00 off of catalog price on your next order of Scott, Foresman and Company Professional Publishing Group business or computer books.

✂

YES, please send me my free catalog of your latest business and computer books!

Name (please print) _____

Company _____

Address _____

City_____ State_____ ZIP_____

Mail response card to: Scott, Foresman and Company
Professional Publishing Group
1900 East Lake Avenue
Glenview, IL 60025

PUBLISHER'S COUPON   NO EXPIRATION DATE

SAVE $1.00

Limit one per order. Good only on Scott, Foresman and Company Professional Publishing Group publications. Consumer pays any sales tax. Coupon may not be assigned, transferred, or reproduced. Coupon will be redeemed by Scott, Foresman and Company, Professional Publishing Group, 1900 East Lake Avenue, Glenview, IL 60025.

Customer's Signature_____